The Microfinance Impact

T0271684

Financial inclusion through microfinance has become a powerful force in improving the living conditions of poor farmers, rural non-farm enterprises and other vulnerable groups. In its unique ability to link the existing extensive network of India's rural bank branches with the Self Help Groups (SHG), the National Bank for Agriculture and Rural Development (NABARD) has covered up to 97 million poor households by March 2010 under its Self Help Group Bank Linkage Programme (SBLP). Policy makers have proclaimed SHGs as 'the most potent initiative ... for delivering financial services to the poor in a sustainable manner'.

This book presents a comprehensive scientific assessment of the impact of the Self Help Group Bank Linkage Programme on the member households. The book discusses wide-ranging topics, including the rural financial sector in India, the history and structure of the SBLP, the impact methodologies, the economic and social impact of microfinance, its role in building assets while reducing poverty and vulnerability, the role of women and their empowerment, training and accumulation of human capital and policy implications of lessons learned.

The empirical results show that vulnerability of the more mature SHG members declines significantly. Vulnerability also falls for villages with better infrastructure and for SHGs that are formed by non-governmental organizations (NGOs) and linked by banks. The results strongly demonstrate that, on average, there is a significant increase in the empowerment of the female participants. The economic impact of SBLP is found to be the most empowering. Greater autonomy and changes in social attitudes also lead to female empowerment. The investigation further reveals that training (especially business training) has a definite positive impact on assets but not on income. The impact of training can be improved through better infrastructure (as in paved roads), linkage model type and the training organiser.

Bridging the gap in the existing literature between academics and practitioners, this book moves beyond the usual theoretical issues in the impact assessment literature and draws on new developments in methodology. It will be of interest to academics, development practitioners and students of economics, political science, sociology, public policy and development studies.

Ranjula Bali Swain is Associate Professor at the Department of Economics at Uppsala University, Sweden.

Routledge studies in development economics

The Microfinance Impact

Ranjula Bali Swain

LONDON AND NEW YORK

First published 2012
by Routledge
2 Park Square, Milton Park, Abingdon, Oxfordshire OX14 4RN

Simultaneously published in the USA and Canada
by Routledge
711 Third Avenue, New York, NY 10017

First issued in paperback 2014

Routledge is an imprint of the Taylor & Francis Group, an informa business

British Library Cataloguing in Publication Data
A catalogue record for this book is available from the British Library

Library of Congress Cataloging in Publication Data
Bali Swain, Ranjula.
The microfinance impact/by Ranjula Bali Swain.
  p. cm.
  1. Microfinance–India. 2. SHG–Bank Linkage Programme (India) 3.
Self-help groups–India. I. Title.
  HG178.33.I4B35 2012
  332–dc23
                                                      2011049074
ISBN 978-0-415-61723-9 (hbk)
ISBN 978-1-138-80837-9 (pbk)
ISBN 978-0-203-11815-3 (ebk)

Typeset in Times New Roman
by Wearset Ltd, Boldon, Tyne and Wear

For B.M.

Contents

Figures

Tables

Preface

We were all waiting in silence! Meeting a newly formed Self Help Group (SHG) in rural Orissa, I had just asked the members their names, as we were introduced. Several more uncomfortable minutes of unresponsiveness passed. An experienced banker then quietly explained that conditioned by the norms of the society, their given names had fallen into disuse as they were addressed as 'wife of X' or 'mother of Y', etc. They lacked the self-confidence to even speak up their names in public. Pointing towards the articulate and confident woman micro-entrepreneur from another SHG, he informed me that three years back she had given him the same response. The transformation was remarkable! Over the years and several field visits later, it was obvious that the Self Help Group Bank Linkage Programme (SBLP) was changing several lives through providing microfinance and related services. This book is a scientific investigation of this impact.

'Self help is the best help' is an old adage. Tentatively piloted by the National Bank for Agriculture and Rural Development (NABARD), the SBLP has covered over 97 million households, as of March 2010. Unique in its ability to utilize India's huge rural banking network and combining it with the democratic, autonomous and flexible features of the Self Help Group, the SBLP harnessed India's non-government organizations, government agencies and banking sector to link the two. In Budget 2012, India's Finance Minister announced that the government proposes to table the Micro Finance Institutions (Development and Regulation) Bill, in the Budget Session of the Parliament. An interest rate subvention to the women self-help groups was also proposed. The Indian government continues to invest resources in SBLP, promoting it as one of its prime strategies for poverty alleviation, financial inclusion and women empowerment. Is this justified? This book conducts an impact assessment of the SBLP at the household level and attempts to answer this question.

Acknowledgements

My accumulated debt in writing this book has been augmented through the support and help of several individuals in the last ten years. The Department of Economics, Uppsala University, Sweden, has been the perfect home for this work. My thanks go to all the Department colleagues who provided a stimulating research environment. I am particularly grateful to Anders Klevmarken, Per-Anders Edin, Bertil Holmlund, Nils Gottfries, Per Johansson, Javad Amid and Chuan-Zhong Li for their inputs and support. The research grant from the Swedish Agency for Research Cooperation with Developing Countries (SAREC) that has financed a part of this research and funded the implementation of the Self Help Group Impact Assessment Survey (SIAS), is gratefully acknowledged. A special thanks to Nivedita Scudder, Rashmi Mohanty and Bhanu Prasad Panigrahi at Unnayan, Bhubaneswar, who along with Bikram, Mihir, the supervisors, surveyors and translators were instrumental in implementing SIAS in the field.

The Microfinance Impact has resulted from the aggregated research findings that I have published, sometimes with co-authors, in journals, edited books, monograph and research reports since 2002. Research that I have co-authored with Adel Varghese, Maria Floro and Fan Yang Wallentin has been incorporated into this book in several chapters as mentioned in those chapters' endnotes. For the stimulating intellectual discussions and arguments, academic partnership and their generous friendship, I remain deeply grateful.

The National Bank for Agriculture and Rural Development (NABARD) has been equally cooperative in sharing their information and knowledge and in accepting my criticism. I remain especially grateful to the Chairman of NABARD, Dr Prakash Bakshi, who was instrumental in initiating my interest in SBLP. Thanks are also due to Y.C. Nanda, H.R. Dave, Dr V. Puhazhendhi, K.M. Rao, Krishna Jindal, B.S. Suran, P.P. Basu Choudhury, S. Sankara Narayanan, M.S. Misra, S. Pattnaik and to the staff at NABARD's head office in Mumbai and the Regional offices at Bhubaneswar and Chennai.

The Swedish International Development Cooperation Agency (Sida) has always shown interest in my research, especially the Department for Infrastructure and Economic Cooperation and Division for Market Development. I would especially like to thank Camilla Bengtsson and Ola Sahlen for their support at Sida. Others who have contributed valuable help are Raghav Gaiha, Neerja Jayal, Marek Hudon, Marc Labie, Ariane Szafarz, Lopa Mudra Tripathy, Sanjoy Pattnaik, Sirje Pädam, Ann-Sofie Djerf Wettergren and Åke Qvarfort. Earlier versions of this book have been presented at different institutions and international conferences. I profited much from the constructive and thoughtful comments from those attending the presentations. I would also like to thank my students, whose questions and comments in the classroom and seminars have brought clarity to the ideas and arguments in the book.

With loving gratitude, I thank my parents, Bou and Ravina, my sister, who have selflessly supported me through various challenges in life and during all phases of this work. My children, Kabir and Simran, through their affection and love have turned the most mundane moments into joy. And Ashok, who has been a partner, a friend, a support and an inspiration – thank you!

Abbreviations

AGM	Assistant General Manager
AMS	Andhra Mahila Sabha
ATM	automated teller machine
APRACA	Asia-Pacific Rural and Agricultural Credit Association
ATT	average treatment effect on treated
BC	Business Correspondent Model
BF	Business Facilitator Model
BPL	Below Poverty Line
BRAC	Bangladesh Rural Advancement Committee
CIA	conditional independence/unconfoundedness assumption
CMF	Centre for Microfinance
DCCB	District Central Cooperative Bank
DDM	District Development Manager
DGM	Deputy General Manager
DRDA	District Rural Development Agency
DWCRA	Development of Women and Children in Rural Areas
FGD	focus group discussion
FGT	Foster-Greer-Thorbecke
FWWB	Friends of Women's World Banking
GTZ	Deutsche Gesellschaft für Technische Zusammenarbeit
HDI	Human Development Index
ICDS	Integrated Child Development Society
ICICI	Industrial Credit and Investment Corporation of India
IRDP	Integrated Rural Development Programme
LLR	local linear regression
MACS	Mutually Aided Cooperative Society
Mcid	Microcredit Innovation Department (at NABARD)
MDG	Millennium Development Goals
MFI	Microfinance Institution
MFO	microfinance organization

MPI	microfinance penetration index
MPPI	microfinance poverty penetration index
MYRADA	Professional Assistance for Development Action and Mysore Resettlement and Development Agency
NA	Nazareth Ashram
NABARD	National Bank for Agriculture and Rural Development
NBFC	non-bank finance company
NCAER	National Council for Applied Economic Research
NGO	non-governmental organization
NN	nearest neighbour matching algorithm
NSSO	National Sample Survey Organization
PACS	primary agricultural credit society
PDS	Public Distribution System
PRADAN	Professional Assistance for Development Action
PSM	propensity score matching
RBI	Reserve Bank of India
REDP	Rural Entrepreneurial Development Programme
RRB	Regional Rural Bank
SBLP	SHG–Bank Linkage Programme
SC	scheduled caste
SEM	structural equation model
SGSY	Swarnajayanti Gram Swarozgar Yojana
SHG	Self Help Group
SHPA	Self Help Promotion Agency
SHPI	Self Help Promoting Institution
SIAS	Self Help Group Impact Assessment Survey
SIDBI	Small Industries Development Bank of India
ST	scheduled tribe
THADCO	Tamil Nadu Adi Dravidar Housing and Development Corporation
TNCDW	Tamil Nadu Corporation for the Development of Women
TRYSEM	Training of Rural Youth for Self Employment
W&CD	Women and Child Development Department, Government of Orissa

1   The Self Help Group Bank Linkage Programme

Introduction

With the mission 'to promote sustainable and equitable agriculture and rural prosperity through effective credit support, related services, institutional development and other innovative initiatives', the National Bank for Agriculture and Rural Development[1] (NABARD) piloted the Self Help Group Bank Linkage Programme in India in 1992. By 31 March 2010, there were about seven million savings linked Self Help Groups (SHG) and more than 4.9 million credit linked SHGs covering 97 million poor households under microfinance programme.

The Reserve Bank of India (RBI) estimates that in India about 40 per cent of the people remain excluded from financial services, of which a large percentage is poor and disadvantaged. This is mainly due to the limited presence of banks in the rural areas. Based on different reports and surveys of the RBI, it is estimated that only 40 per cent of the adult population has access to a savings account, about 5.2 per cent of the villages have a bank branch, and about 97.7 million small farmers are covered by farm credit.[2]

The majority of India's rural poor remain dependent on agriculture for their primary source of income and a majority of them are marginal or small farmers, whereas the poorest amongst them are landless (Basu 2006). Morduch and Rutherford (2003) argue that the poor people value financial services and want these to be reliable, convenient, continuous, and flexible. But the rural borrowers find that the rural banks do not provide flexible products and services to meet the income and expenditure patterns of small rural borrowers. Furthermore, the transaction costs of dealing with formal banks are high, especially given the complex procedures and the corruption involved. Together, these factors raise the cost of loans for the borrowers and it takes a long time before the loans are approved. Many rural borrowers are also constrained as they lack land as a collateral and thus have difficulty getting loans (Bali Swain 2002).

Banks do not want to serve poor high-risk, high-cost clients, because of uncertainty about their repayment capacity, their volatile income and expenditure patterns. Lack of collateral magnifies these existing problems. The transaction costs of rural lending are also very high due to the small loan size, the high frequency of transactions, the geographically spread clientele, the heterogeneity of borrowers and illiteracy. In India, government policies like 'priority sector' lending targets;[3] interest rate restrictions (floors on short-term deposit rates and ceilings on lending impose an 'implicit tax' on banks) and the interference from the government in the Regional Rural Banks (RRBs) and cooperative banks further aggravates the problem.

The 2001 Census of India revealed that only about 30 per cent of the rural population in India had access to banking services (savings or credit through the formal banking system). In the states of Andhra Pradesh and Uttar Pradesh about 41 per cent of rural households had a bank savings account and 21 per cent had taken a bank loan (World Bank and National Council of Applied Economic Research 2003). Comparing these figures to the poverty estimates for rural India of 25–50 per cent, Sinha *et al.* (2009) conclude that there are more excluded from the banking sector than there are poor, which implies that there is considerable scope to expand outreach of financial services to a wide range of rural population in India.

Reviewing the All India Debt and Investment Survey 1981–82, NABARD concluded that the rural financial system had not achieved its objectives. Motivated by the Asia-Pacific Rural and Agricultural Credit Association (APRACA), NABARD implemented a pilot study in 1987. The results were encouraging, and the Self Help Group Bank Linkage Programme (SBLP) was implemented as a pilot programme and mainstreamed in 1996. Subsequently, the programme has grown to dominate the microfinance sector in India and remains one of the largest microfinance programmes in the world.

According to the global survey by Economist Intelligence Unit (2009) the microfinance sector in India is the fourth most organized amongst 54 countries. Broadly the microfinance sector is defined as direct customers of banks for small loans, small and vulnerable members of primary cooperative credit societies, SHG members and clients of microfinance institutions (MFIs). There are more than 800 MFIs in India, of which the top 20 account for about 95 per cent of their aggregate loan portfolio (Allen *et al.* 2007). Major alternative MFIs in India are: the Small Industries Development Bank of India (SIDBI) Foundation for Micro-Credit (SFMC) – the largest lender of the emerging MFIs; Friends of Women's World Banking, India (FWWB-I); SHARE Microfinance Ltd; Span Dana; and National Women's Fund (Rashtriya Mahila Kosh, in Hindi). Basu (2006) suggests that their outreach is modest due to several reasons. Their growth remains constrained by a legal and regulatory framework as they have been restricted to mobilize member deposits, equity, and raise debt from external sources for a large part. Further limitations arise from the lack of adequate capacity and skills in financial control and management, management information systems (MIS), new product design, etc.

Additional efforts involve partnerships between private banks and service providers. These mostly include the Industrial Credit and Investment Corporation of India (ICICI) bank, Unit Trust of India (UTI) bank and Housing Development Finance Corporation (HDFC) bank. Rapid expansion of commercial bank lending to the Indian microfinance sector from 2004 has resulted in fast growth of MFIs. A major contributor to this expansion was the 'Partnership Model' by ICICI bank, under which the loans to borrowers remain on the books of the bank, off the balance sheet of the MFI partner. Thus, under this model the MFI partner performs the social intermediation whereas the bank bears the credit risk. Although the MFI partly shares the risk of default by providing a 'first loss guarantee', this model removes the MFI's equity and on-lending funds constraints. For provision of agricultural credit (mostly crop loans), the Kisan Credit Card (KCC) was launched in 1998–99 by the commercial banks, RRBs and cooperative banks. Its main objective was to reduce borrowers' and transaction costs as well as delays in accessing and renewing crop loans.

Ghate *et al.* (2007) estimate that around 22 per cent of all poor households were receiving microcredit and microfinance services. About half of SHG members and 30 per cent of MFI members were estimated to be poor. In order to find out more about the extent of the outreach of Indian microfinance Srinivasan (2010) estimates two separate indices. The microfinance penetration index (MPI), which is computed by dividing the share of the microfinance clients with the share of population, shows a clear southern bias. Three of the top five states are in the south and have a high MPI: Andhra Pradesh (3.64), Tamil Nadu (2.77) and Karnataka (1.57). While the MPI measures whether the client acquisition in different states is proportional to the population, the intensity of penetration of microfinance among poor index (MPPI) measures this with respect to the population of poor households. The MPPI is the ratio of the share of the state in microfinance clients to the share of the state in population of poor. Again four out of the top five states in terms of their MPPI are the southern states of Andhra Pradesh (6.35), Tamil Nadu (2.77), Kerala (2.49) and Karnataka (1.74).

Banking sector and rural finance in India

Indigenous finance with components of microfinance dates back to before the first millennium BC in India.[4] During the 1950s about 80 per cent of the Indian population lived in rural areas, with agriculture contributing 40 per cent to the GDP. However, only 2.2 per cent of the total credit went to agriculture, of which the majority accrued to big farmers (Seibel 2010). According to the rural indebtedness surveys of Reserve Bank of India (RBI), informal credit accounted for 90 per cent (70 per cent) of rural indebtedness in 1951 (1971).

With predominantly agriculture dependent new emerging low income states after the Second World War, rural finance was made the priority, with large state agricultural banks lending subsidized credit to farmers in India and across various developing countries in the world. The intention was to enable the farmers to make investments (for irrigation, fertilizers, adoption of new crop varieties and technology) to increase agricultural productivity (Bali Swain 2001; Armendáriz and Morduch 2010).

Since the very beginning the Indian government has emphasized improving access to financial services with the objective of providing agricultural capital and reducing poverty (RBI 1954). The commercial banks were nationalized making it mandatory for them to provide subsidiary credit during the aggressive rural banking drive of the 1970s and 1980s. By the 1990s there was a partial deregulation of interest rates, a gradual reduction in the government's stake in commercial banks, and increased competition in the banking sector (Basu 2006).

Fisher *et al.* (2002) discuss the three phases in the development of the financial sector of India. During the first phase until the 1960s, the developmental objectives were pursued through the financial sector with the focus on delivering agricultural credit through cooperatives. The second phase was the nationalization of 14 commercial banks in 1969 (and another six banks in 1980), a requirement that banks were obliged to open two rural branches for every urban branch and a mandatory system of priority sector lending to the disadvantaged sectors of the economy. When the failure of cooperatives and the ineffectiveness of the rural branches of large commercial banks became apparent, a network of RRBs was established in the 1970s, resulting in one of the largest bank networks in the world.

Between 1977 and 1991, the Indian central bank (RBI) mandated that for every branch opened in an already banked location a commercial bank must open four in unbanked locations, thus creating one of the largest rural branch expansion programmes in the world (Burgess and Pandey 2005). Investigating the poverty impact of access to finance, Burgess and Pandey find that between the bank nationalization in 1969 and the onset of financial liberalization in 1990 bank branches were opened in over 30,000 rural locations which had no prior presence of commercial banks. Their estimates suggest that a 1 per cent increase in the number of rural locations banked per capita reduced rural poverty by 0.42 per cent and increased total output by 0.34 per cent (Fisher *et al.* 2002). The proportion of rural credit from the formal financial sector (banks and cooperatives) rose from 29.2 per cent in 1971 to 61.2 per cent in 1981, but declined to 56.6 per cent by 1991.

The government of India also instituted the Integrated Rural Development Programme (IRDP) in 1980–81 to provide direct subsidized loans to poor self-employed people through the banking sector reaching about 55 million families over two decades. According to Armendáriz and Morduch (2010), IRDP is the perfect example of an inefficient subsidized credit programme. The programme allocated about 30 per cent of the loans towards socially excluded groups (scheduled caste and scheduled tribe). About \$6 billion (25 per cent to 50 per cent of loan volume) was allocated to the weaker sectors in subsidies between 1979 and 1989. The IRDP repayment rate was 60 per cent, with only 11 per cent of borrowers taking a second loan (Pulley 1989). By 2000, the IRDP loan recovery rate fell to just 31 per cent (Meyer 2002).

The second phase ended in 1989 with the first official loan waiver that severely undermined the remnants of the credit discipline. Fisher *et al.* (2002) note that with the start of the financial crisis of the early 1990s which led to significant economic liberalization – including reforms in the financial sector – the third phase kicked in. This included slow restructuring of the commercial and regional rural banks, the freeing of some interest rates, the consolidation of the government's self-employment schemes (Swarnajayanti Gram Swarozgar Yojana (SGSY)), the introduction of local area banks, mutually aided cooperative societies (MACS) autonomous of government control, and other measures. The reforms of the financial sector made things worse for the poor. According to Karmakar (1999: 108–109) there was a drastic fall in the share of cooperatives in rural credit. The share of rural credit in the total credit disbursed by commercial banks, which grew from 3.5 to 15 per cent from 1971 to 1991, declined to 11 per cent in 1998 (Sa-Dhan 2001).

India still has an enviable formal financial infrastructure with 32,000 rural branches of commercial banks (mostly public sector commercial banks) and regional rural banks, about 14,000 cooperative bank branches, 98,000 primary agricultural credit societies (PACS), thousands of mutual fund sellers, several non-bank finance companies (NBFCs), and a large post office network[5] with 154,000 outlets that are required to focus on deposit mobilization and money transfers (Basu 2006). However, a large majority of India's rural poor do not have access to formal finance and remain credit constrained (Bali Swain 2002). According to Basu (2006), 66 per cent of large farmers have a deposit account while about 44 per cent have access to credit.

Self Help Group Bank Linkage Programme

Analysing the data of the All-India Debt and Investment Survey, NAB-ARD's research unit in 1983 concluded that the rural financial system had failed to reach its objectives. It concluded that the procedures of the rural banks were unduly complicated and costly. The emphasis on production loans was considered ill-guided by them as the existing loan products did not meet the needs of the rural poor. The poor were able to save but did not have the opportunity of depositing their savings. Moreover, the transaction costs were high and the financial products were unsuitable for the intended clients. This resulted in NABARD realizing that their programmes had to be savings and not credit oriented and that the poor have to have a say in the product design (Seibel 2006).

Around the mid 1980s the Asia-Pacific Rural and Agricultural Credit Association (APRACA), an association of Asian agricultural and central banks, was experimenting with the linkage banking model (Seibel 2010). In 1986 SHG banking was adopted as an APRACA programme. Implementing a recommendation made by APRACA, a study was carried out in 1987 by NABARD where the Self Help Groups were piloted (Seibel 2006). This first survey on SHGs conducted an action research on linking SHGs with the concept of savings and credit in 1987 and published the outcome of the research in the form of a survey report in 1989 (NCAER 2008).[6] NABARD, along with some NGOs (Andhra Mahila Sabha (AMS), Kerala Gandhi Samarak Nidhi (KGSN), Nazareth Ashram (NA) and Professional Assistance for Development Action and Mysore Resettlement and Development Agency (MYRADA)), piloted the linkage model and coordinated a field study of SHGs in 1987. Recovery of these loans was excellent, with a positive impact on bonded labour. Studies carried out by NABARD in the mid 1980s confirmed that the immediate needs of financial services for the poor were: the possibility to secure their micro savings; access to consumption loans to meet emergency needs; and relatively simple financial services and products, including loans for microenterprises. In the late 1980s NABARD suggested that the programmes for the poor should be savings-led and not credit driven (NCAER 2008).

The Grameen Bank model was also discussed in the Indian Parliament as a new banking structure. However, based on NABARD's studies and inspired by its linkage experience under APRACA, NABARD instead argued for the Self Help Group Bank Linkage approach. This programme had the advantage of using the existing infrastructure of banks and social organizations, focusing on savings and using banks rather than donor resources in the provision of credit (Seibel 2010). Reviewing the situation of rural finance in India[7] and based on its recent experience NABARD suggested the need to adopt a new approach where the existing rural formal infrastructure of banks could be used with the help of social organizations to provide financial services (especially savings) to the rural poor.

Between 1989 and 1991, NABARD entered into a policy dialogue with RBI to make preparations for a pilot project linking informal groups to banks. The guidelines of APRACA's Indonesian project were found useful, but were adjusted to the Indian context. The Indian government had early on identified the potential of the SHGs given the existing network of rural banks and vibrant NGO sector. Discussions between NABARD and RBI resulted in a pilot project where informal groups could be linked to banks (NABARD 1991). To facilitate this further, RBI advised the commercial banks to participate actively in a non-mandatory pilot project refinanced by NABARD (RBI 1991). The pilot phase was implemented between 1992 and 1996 by MYRADA (in Karnataka) and Professional Assistance for Development Action[8] (PRADAN) (in Rajasthan, Tamil Nadu and Jharkhand) with strong support from NABARD in the early 1990s with 500 SHGs.

The programme was mainstreamed in 1996, with NABARD providing refinancing to participating banks. SHG banking was declared the dominant but non-mandatory approach of lending to the poor with the intention to credit link about one million SHGs by 2008 and setting up the Micro Credit Innovations Department with cells in all states of India. Legal flaws were removed[9] and detailed guidelines were issued along with recommendations from a RBI constituted Working Group that investigated several issues concerning SHGs and NGOs (RBI 1996). A special fund was created to refinance capacity building measures, establishments were assisted to maintain SHGs through numerous NGOs and government organizations were promoted and initiatives to organize SHGs into cooperative federations under new state laws were allowed. Overall the SBLP was supported by the joint political will of union government, state governments, the RBI and NABARD (Seibel 2010).

Nair (2005) notes that SBLP allows the SHGs to obtain loans from banks – commercial, rural and cooperative banks. These banks are further eligible for subsidized refinance from NABARD.[10] SBLP has been effective in terms of significant outreach with repayment rates of over 95 per cent as compared to other poverty lending programmes with repayment rates of 50 per cent. SHGs banking was highly profitable, even with deregulated lending rates of 10 to 13 per cent, as transaction costs were low and the reported recovery rates were 98 per cent (Seibel and Dave 2002). With increased bankers' confidence in SHG banking, banks started using their own resources and NABARD's refinancing dropped from 91 per cent in 1999 to 33 per cent in 2007 (Seibel 2010).

Innovating with the decaying system NABARD created a new approach and product to serve India's rural poor. Isern *et al.* (2007), however, argue that the dominant factor behind lending to SHGs under the SBLP was the government mandated lending targets of 40 per cent of total bank credit to borrowers from priority sectors, including agriculture, microfinance, small industry, housing and education. Of this, 10 per cent had to be extended to 'economically weaker sections'. These targets were monitored by senior bank managers and government officials, who were answerable to Members of Parliament. However, a few commercial banks engaged in SHGs as they found them profitable.

During the initial period, the growth of SBLP was slow due to multiple factors. According to Nair (2005), unlike other subsidized lending programmes supported by the government, SBLP was not mandatory for the banks. Promoting and linking the SHGs required a substantial amount of institutional learning and human resources. This was especially important since the organization-based lending mechanism of SHG was different from the individual and activity-based lending that the bankers were familiar with. Another constraint was the lack of suitable promoters in the field with the capacity to link the SHGs to the banks. To determine credit worthiness the bankers were supposed to judge the SHGs on their proper account maintenance and regular group meetings. Performance of loan repayment on the internal lending was also used to determine their creditworthiness. Finally, SBLP required collateral-free lending which was an alien concept for most bank loans.

The SBLP outreach gradually increased with self-learning and NABARD's extended extensive training programmes to all the actors involved. NABARD organized and financed over 2,000 programmes for bankers and over 250 programmes for NGOs and government functionaries (Nair 2005).

The Self Help Group usually consists of 15 to 20 women, and initially engages in saving and intra-group lending. After six months, SHGs become eligible for a bank loan to the group. An assessment is carried out by the bank or the Self Help Promoting Institution (SHPI) that evaluates the regularity of savings, meetings, internal lending, repayments and records. Once the SHPI is satisfied with the SHG's performance it links the group to a bank (usually the rural branch of a commercial bank, but also RRBs, cooperative banks, etc.). The banks are refinanced by NABARD at slightly subsidized rates.

The SHPIs help motivate, promote and monitor SHGs. There are several models that do this. Typically, grassroots level NGOs link the SHGs to the banks. However, rural branches of commercial banks, cooperative banks, RRBs and non-banking finance companies (NBFCs) may also act as SHPIs linking directly to the SHGs. SHPIs initiate SHG formation by holding the initial information meetings and encouraging creation of the SHGs. They also link the group to the bank, implement saving behaviour and teach the basic accounting skills to the group members. As facilitators they earn a small commission and/or bonus for group repayment and creation of new groups, and are involved in both pre- and post-linkage monitoring. As facilitators they may attend regular group meetings and support the group in various activities including training and skills development (Basu 2006). These are discussed in greater detail in the next section.

Banks lend to the group without collateral, relying on self-monitoring, joint liability and peer pressure for repayment. The initial bank loans have a loans-to-savings ratio of 1 : 1 or 2 : 1, then it is gradually increased to 4 : 1. SHGs that demonstrate good financial discipline are sometimes provided with loans to about ten times their savings. The first bank loan to a SHG usually starts at Rs.10,000, with a repayment period of six months to one year. On repayment of previous loans, larger loan amounts of Rs.25,000, subsequently increasing up to Rs.200,000, are lent with longer pay-back periods (between three and five years).

Members typically save small amounts of Rs.40–50 ($1) a month to group savings. Loans from this fund and from the bank can then be made to members for businesses such as petty trading, but also for consumption and family needs such as school, medical costs or wedding celebrations (Sinha *et al.* 2009).

Not all SHGs pay interest on the savings and there is a wide variation in the interest paid on the member savings. NCAER (2008) finds that it varies between 3.5 to 15 per cent but on average it is about 7 to 8 per cent. In the states of Maharashtra (west) and Uttar Pradesh (centre), more than 95 per cent of the SHGs paid interest on the savings of their group members, whereas in Orissa (east) only 17 per cent of the SHGs paid interest on the savings.

Banks charge an interest rate of 8 to 12 per cent per annum on the loans to SHGs. Amongst the group, the members are free to decide the interest rate charged to its members. The NCAER (2008) study found that the SHGs typically charged about 24 per cent per annum (about 2 to 3 per cent per month) to their group members, such that the rates would be below those of moneylenders but high enough to discourage unnecessary loans. Penal rates were also charged on overdue loans to enforce timely repayments. The group is also free to decide its repayment schedule, etc. within the group. The loans may be used for both consumption (health, marriages, other ceremonies, etc.) and investment (individual or group). SBLP interest rates may also have an impact on other interest rates in the market. For instance, in Rayagada district of Orissa, the SBLP has been able to bring down the interest rates on loans by the local informal moneylenders by about 10–20 per cent.[11]

NCAER (2008) finds that about 71 per cent of the SHGs provide loans and services to members once a month. On average SHGs met at about 1.6 times per month and fortnightly meetings were quite common. According to their survey about 90 per cent of the members attended the group meetings and about 80 per cent actively participated in the group discussions. A majority (90 per cent) of the SHGs had their rules and regulations written down, with 43 per cent of them reporting awareness about the objectives amongst their members. Predominantly it is the literate members of the SHG that maintain the record of the group meetings and the account book of the group and the member's passbook. These members usually receive their training from the promoter of the SHPIs. About 26 per cent of the surveyed SHGs had developed financial skills among the members.

NCAER (2008) find that the group leader was nominated in 80 per cent of their survey SHGs while elections were held for only 10 per cent of the cases. SHGs mostly prefer the highest educated amongst their group as the leader. Change in leadership within the group is recommended to spread the leadership experience across other members. The NCAER study further finds that more than 80 per cent of SHGs change their leader at least once or twice a year. Investigating the rotation of leadership in four districts of Andhra Pradesh, a study by NABARD finds that there was limited change in leadership and book-keeping was not updated (Srinivasan 2010).

According to Sinha *et al.* (2009), the overall dropout rate of SHG members is less than 10 per cent. SHG members dropped out mainly due to migration from the village and financial difficulties. When the SHG members leave their groups they are supposed to receive their savings deposit plus accumulated interest rate, minus repayment of any overdue, however full payment of interest is not always made.

The NCAER (2008) study also reports a dropout rate of 8.2 per cent (or on average one person per group). According to it, members dropped out of the groups due to lack of benefits from SHGs (44 per cent of SHGs), migration of the member (29 per cent), illness (8 per cent), etc. About 15 per cent of the members dropped out because of default in making savings or repayments, while another 15 per cent exited due to non-availability of loan. The net dropout effect was buffered by the new members that joined the group.

In effect SHGs are microbanks that are self-managed by their members, who mobilize their funds from different sources and use them as they decide (Sinha *et al.* 2009). The SHGs independently determine how much each member saves; they keep their own records and decide which member shall borrow, how much and at what rate of interest and how often they should meet.

SHGs that are on the Below Poverty Line (BPL) list are eligible for the central government's Swarnajayanti Gram Swarozgar Yojana (SGSY) and can apply for subsidized loans under it. These loans have a substantial subsidy element (30–50 per cent of the loan) and start from Rs.25,000. But subsequent loans can increase quickly up to Rs.300,000. The size of the loan, the subsidized credit and the way it is administered by the banks make the SGSY a distinctly different programme from microfinance.

Under this strategy SHGs were funded to perform a few identified activities at the block level. The disbursement of the government funds was made through the DRDAs (District Rural Development Agencies) that distributed the subsidies to the banks. The programme was implemented with close interaction between the government officials at various levels, including the DRDAs, managers of the participating banks, NABARD and NGOs. After the first 6 months of group formation, under SGSY the group becomes eligible for a revolving fund of Rs.25,000 from a participating bank. Rs.10,000 of this loan is the subsidy component, thus the bank may charge interest only on the remaining amount. Six months after this the group is tested for its ability to take up economic activities. If it passes then the group is eligible for loan and subsidy for economic activity up to a maximum of Rs.10,000 per group member or Rs.125,000 per group, whichever is less. Besides financing and identifying activities, SGSY also needs to recognize and provide the training and building capacity of the participating members and groups (Nair 2005). However, the sustainability and the quality of SHGs promoted under this programme are suspect. Some state governments like Andhra Pradesh made SHGs their main strategy in rural development, thus inducing several government agencies to form SHGs.

As of March 2002 the SHG programme had covered about 461,478 SHGs with a cumulative lending of Rs.10,260 million and accumulated savings in SHGs of Rs.8,750 million. About 90 per cent of the financed SHGs were exclusively women. In all, 444 banks, of which 121 were rural regional banks, 209 cooperative banks, all 27 public sector banks and 17 private banks with a total of 17,085 branches, participated in the programme, providing credit to about 7.8 million poor households in 488 districts. Average loan sizes were Rs.22,240 per SHG and Rs.1,300 per member. Since the very beginning the state-wise distribution of SHGs showed a southern focus. Andhra Pradesh accounted for 42 per cent of all linked SHGs. This figure was 12 per cent for Tamil Nadu and 9 per cent for Karnataka. Loans outstanding[12] under SBLP as of March 2005 was about 59 per cent of the cumulative lending (Ramakrishna 2006) and about 71 per cent for the SHGs that had been linked till that point (Ghate *et al.* 2007).

The women-only SHGs that were credit linked with banks in 2009–10 were 81.6 per cent whereas those that were savings linked were nearly 76.4 per cent. As of 31 March 2009, about 82 per cent of the amount of loans were outstanding to women SHGs (NABARD 2009).

At the end of March 2010, about 4.5 million SHGs had outstanding loans with a volume of Rs.273 billion in outstanding loans (Srinivasan 2010). SLBP accounts for nearly 88.5 million savers and remains an important provider of saving services to the formerly financially excluded. As of 31 March 2010, the share of bank loans outstanding to SHGs, as a percentage of loans outstanding to weaker sections by scheduled commercial banks, was 16.3 per cent (NABARD 2011). By 2010, the number of SHGs (volume of loans to SHGs) from the commercial banks accounted for nearly 67 per cent (68 per cent), whereas RRBs' share was 22 per cent (21 per cent) and cooperative banks' was 11 per cent (11 per cent) (Srinivasan 2010).

About 6.81 million groups had saved with the SBLP by the end of March 2010. Of the total amount saved 58 per cent of the SHG savings were with the commercial banks, 20 per cent with the RRBs and 22 per cent with the cooperative banks. However, one-third of the savings linked groups did not get a credit linkage till the end of March 2010. Commercial banks had a much higher share of borrowing groups but a smaller share of savings groups, whereas the cooperatives have both a higher share of number of groups that saved and also the amount of money that was saved. However, the SBLP has started showing a declining trend in both outreach and loan portfolio recently (Srinivasan 2010).

Comparing the Grameen Bank to the SBLP, it is obvious that both create trust or social capital based on joint liability. However, unlike the Grameen bank style implementation that is top to bottom driven, has a fixed structure and offers limited scope for variation, the SHGs, which are catalysed through external promoting institutions (primarily NGOs), are largely autonomous in their functioning. Harper (2002) argues that the Self Help Groups are flexible, do not require banks, and are highly empowering. They are relatively free from different institutions and there is no prestructured loan ladder. They also have the freedom to evolve from existing groups into federations and cooperatives. However, on the downside, the groups lack proper management skills and time to update book-keeping, are susceptible to internal and external capture (domination or influence) and cash may not be secure.

From the institutional perspective, SHGs involve lower transaction costs and can be linked to an existing financial institution, but they are harder to monitor and may be tempted by other banks or by politicians. For the SBLP programme to be effective, Harper (2002) argues that it takes NGOs or highly committed staff to develop groups and thus the development of the SBLP is relatively slow.

Self Help Promoting Institutions

The SHG programme links with the poor through Self Help Promoting Institutions (SHPIs), which primarily includes NGOs, but also banks and government officials. The agencies survey the village, provide the details of the programme, enlist borrowers and sometimes organize the training. Three types of linkages have emerged as the most common. In linkage model 1, banks both form and finance SHGs. According to NABARD (2006), roughly 20 per cent of SHGs fall under this linkage model. In the most popular linkage model 2 (roughly three-fourths of all SHGs), NGOs and others form the groups but banks directly finance them. In the third linkage model banks finance the SHGs through NGOs (but only 5 per cent of linkages fall under this model).[13]

For NGOs, SHG promotion usually started as a part of a village development programme, covering issues of land, watershed, forestry, livelihoods and sanitation. Several NGOs started groups for men and women, with the objective of increasing their participation in planning and managing resources. SHGs were also perceived as a vehicle for promoting women's development, participation and empowerment.

Sinha *et al.* (2009) argue that for governmental programmes, SHGs became a means to achieve a larger development agenda. For instance, some government programmes like Swa-Shakti and other development schemes implemented by District Rural Development Agencies (DRDAs) promoted income-generation activities for women through SHGs. SHGs were also aggressively promoted by some social programmes, such as the Integrated Child Development Services and the Development of Women and Children in Rural Areas (DWCRA) scheme in the 1990s by the state government of Andhra Pradesh. The bank's interest in promoting linkages for SHG lending was mainly motivated by lending in line with priority sector guidelines for the banking sector. Although banks may directly link to the SHGs, they usually took assistance from local NGOs which provided capacity building and monitoring services for a fee. Sinha *et al.* (2009) find overlap between the different types of SHPIs. Thus, local NGOs may assist bank-promoted groups, government or bank SHPIs sometimes take over SHGs promoted by NGOs, etc.

SHPIs reduced the transaction costs for the banks by taking up credit evaluation, loan monitoring, etc. Peer-pressure from group members ensured higher repayment and hence a lower default (of less than 1 per cent). SHPIs provided training and capacity building to the SHG members. This involved an initial introduction to the self help concept, norms of the group (meetings, savings, lending, interest, instalments, etc.), the role of the group leaders and the type of books maintained for the SHG transactions; this continues over the first four to six group meetings. Group leaders (the president, the secretary and a treasurer) usually received on-the-job training, especially if they are responsible for the group's book-keeping (Sinha *et al.* 2009).

Most SHPIs also provided exposure visits to established SHGs, different types of development support and community-wide initiatives. The inputs of the SHPIs may vary depending on the institutions' objective. According to Sinha *et al.*'s (2009) study about 27 per cent of the SHPIs were focused primarily on microfinance, whereas 21 per cent were focused on both microfinance and development activities. Around 15 per cent of the SHPIs were more oriented towards development and provided little guidance on financial transactions. Other SHPIs provided very limited input on both microfinance and development objectives and conducted only one meeting on SHG norms, with no additional supervision and monitoring services. A majority of such SHPIs were government agencies or banks. In 2000, two-thirds of SHGs in India were linked by NGOs, but by 2007 their share was down to less than one-third with nearly half of them being promoted by the government (Allen *et al.* 2007).

SHG federations[14] were primarily promoted as an exit strategy, to allow SHPIs to withdraw their support from SHGs while also ensuring their sustainability (Srinivasan 2010). SHGs form federations or networks, at the village, village cluster or higher levels. Sinha *et al.* (2009) suggest that in the 1990s, SHG federations were promoted by the NGOs and the state governments with the aim to create institutions that could substitute for the SHPIs' functions and roles. They were expected to facilitate credit access and repayments, in addition to providing women with a structure and platform to negotiate with wider institutions in society. Federations have the possibility to transform into a formal institution and may thus avail direct access to bulk loans from a variety of financial institutions, including banks. Federations were first introduced in the southern states by NGOs but in Orissa they were adopted as part of a government programme for women (Mission Shakti) as a means to disburse bank credit to SHGs.

The growth of MFIs in India was mostly financed by the private sector, which initially lend at the level of priority sector lending obligations. Over time, however, they found lending to MFIs is profitable as they have very high repayment rates. Banks provide term loans and cash credit, charging interest rates in the range of 8.5 to 11 per cent for loans for periods of three months to five years. About 80 per cent of the total outstanding credit from commercial banks is from the Industrial Credit and Investment Corporation of India (ICICI), which is the largest private and second largest bank of India. More than half of this lending (60 per cent) is through the 'partnership model' where MFIs provide social intermediation (loan origination, monitoring and collection services) for a fee. The MFIs also partner in sharing the risk of default. ICICI also lends by buying portfolios of MFIs and charging them an interest of 9 per cent. Technological services like low-cost automated teller machines (ATMs), mobile banking and internet services have also been introduced by ICICI (Allen *et al.* 2007).

Realizing the weakening role of NGOs in the SBLP, the Reserve Bank of India in January 2006 specified the inclusion of the Business Facilitator Model (BFM) and the Business Correspondent Model (BCM) to provide intermediation along with the MFIs. These intermediaries provide services like identifying borrowers, promoting savings, processing and submission of loan and monitoring of repayment. The BFM provide additional services like disbursal of small loans, recovery of principal, collection of interest, sale of micro insurance and mutual fund products. The BFM includes NGOs, cooperatives, post offices, insurance agents and community-based organizations, whereas the BCM includes NGOs and MFIs that are registered under the Trusts Act, not-for-profit companies (Section 25 companies in India) and post offices. These services may be provided for a fee to the banks (Allen *et al.* 2007). In recent years, the RBI has also made incremental changes to include individual shop owners, establishments and petrol pumps as BCs by banks.

Based on the RBI's report of the High Level Committee to Review Lead Bank Scheme[15] (2009), the banks have been asked to prepare a plan for providing banking services in all villages that have remained unbanked thus far and have a population of more than 2,000. The intention behind this is to promote greater financial inclusion. By March 2010, every district had a plan where the public sector bank or a large private sector bank took a leading role. Many of these expansion plans are relying on using BCs as the main way of linking the villagers to the banks. However, the ability of BCs to achieve this is suspect unless they are financially disciplined and have the requisite managerial skills.

Srinivasan (2010) argues that federations might be a way for NABARD to regain leadership of the SBLP. Need-based federations that are facilitated with professional staff and training, and are provided capital for the initial infrastructure, may be developed as community-owned financial institutions by NABARD. Similarly, NABARD can make SHG linkage a core part of the business strategy of cooperative banks and invest in specialized human resources.

To promote and ensure the orderly growth of microfinance services by facilitating the development of policies for transparency, development of rating norms, specifying accounting and auditing norms, the Microfinance Institutions (Development and Regulation) Bill was introduced in the Parliament. It aims to promote and regulate the microfinance sector and to allow the microfinance organizations (MFOs) to collect deposits from 'eligible clients'.[16] The financial assistance to the 'eligible clients' is limited to Rs.50,000 in aggregate per individual for an enterprise, agriculture and allied activities, or up to Rs.150,000 in aggregate per individual for housing purposes. The Microfinance Institutions (Development and Regulation) Bill will make RBI the sole regulator of the Indian microfinance sector. The Finance Minister of India recently announced that the Bill will be tabled in the 2012 Budget Session of the Parliament. The 2012 Budget also proposes an interest subvention to the women SHGs.

2 Impact assessment methodologies and study design[1]

Impact of the SBLP

The Self Help Group Bank Linkage Programme (SBLP) has grown at an accelerated pace. Recent data in India finds that the client outreach has reached 45 million households, three times more than those reached by microfinance institutions (MFIs) (Srinivasan 2009). With the relatively greater outreach, the SHGs have already started showing signs of stagnation (Srinivasan 2011). Still, in 2008–09, SHGs have grown doubly as fast as MFIs (7.2 per cent vs. 4 per cent). With the dominating position of SHGs in the Indian microfinance sector and the government acclaiming the SHG programme as a crucial poverty alleviation strategy, assessing whether SHGs help borrowers has become even more critical. An impact study would find whether SHG membership benefits participating member households and provide information to shape the direction of future policy.

Puhazhendi and Satyasai (2000) was one of the first SHG impact studies conducted by NABARD, to assess the impact of microfinance on the socio-economic conditions of 560 household members from 223 SHGs located in 11 states[2] of India. Using multistage stratified random sampling, the study included SHGs that had completed at least one year of bank linkage as on 31 March 1999. On the basis of a simple pre-post SHG participation comparison, this study found a substantial positive impact on the SHG members. They estimated that the average value of assets per household increased by 72.3 per cent whereas the average SHG household income increased by 33 per cent. The study also found that poverty incidence declined from 42 to 22 per cent, whereas employment increased by 17 per cent between the pre-post SHG phase. Constructing a composite index of socio-economic parameters based on a scoring technique they found the SHG members increased from a score of 45 to 60. They also suggested that SHG participation contributed significantly in improving the self-confidence of the participating women by increasing their sense of self-worth, confidence in confronting social evils and decreasing the incidence of family violence.

Another impact study that has been widely quoted in the policy documents is Puhazhendi and Badatya (2002). Using a sample of 115 members of 60 SHGs from the eastern states of Orissa, Jharkhand and Chattisgarh, this study again relied on the pre-post comparison of the participating SHGs. They found that SHG participation led to an increase in households' assets by 45 per cent, whereas net incomes increased by 23 per cent. The share of Below Poverty Line households declined from 88 to 75 per cent and the employment per household showed a substantial increase of 34 per cent during this period. The SHG participants also reported a substantial improvement in their social empowerment, with an increase in self-confidence, decision making abilities and communication skills. The methodology of the Puhazendhi and Badataya (2002) study, commissioned by NABARD, consisted of computing the percentage difference of the means of members' variables pre and post SHG membership.

Another major SHG impact study was conducted by the National Council of Applied Economic Research (NCAER 2008) with the aims of: assessing the impact of SHG participation on economic activities, household welfare and social empowerment; assessing the quality of the groups promoted by different SHPIs; identifying and assessing the capacity building and training needs of SHGs for income generation activities; finding strategies that make groups more cohesive; evaluating the factors affecting the sustainability of SHGs and the constraints that they face. The study included 4,791 SHG members from 906 functioning mature SHGs that had been linked to the bank for at least four years (2002–07) from six states spread over all the five geographical regions of India: Andhra Pradesh and Karnataka (south); Maharashtra (west); Orissa (east); Uttar Pradesh (Central); Assam (north-east).[3] The reference period for the study was January–December 2006. This study also used the 'before and after' approach to measure the impact of SHG participation by measuring the difference in the compound annual growth rate (CGAR) of a given parameter between pre and post SHG linkage.

Their findings also revealed a very strong impact from SHG participation on a large number of factors. Most of these prominent SHG studies have relied on pre-post methodology, without taking the selection biases into account, which are widely known in the current economics literature.[4] Such wide-scale impact assessments are widely quoted and have a broad policy impact, for instance, the State of the Sector 2008 Report on Indian Microfinance, has no discussion on the methodology. Similarly, the Puhazendhi and Badataya study has had a substantial policy impact and has been referred to by several government reports, most recently by the Rangarajan Committee on Financial Inclusion (RBI 2008).The EDA Rural Systems (2006) report based on 214 SHGs from 108 villages, which is also not a formal impact study, is also referred to as an impact study by the Rangarajan Committee report. It is important to critically reassess the impact studies in terms of their methods to provide a more accurate estimation of the evaluation of the SBLP. Bali Swain and Varghese (2010a) discuss the limitations of the NCAER report in greater detail.

A pre-post methodology does not appropriately account for the changes that SHG member households face. However, identifying a comparison or control group which has not received the benefits of SHG membership but which has experienced the same changes as the treatment group (SHG members), captures the change. Assume one has both baseline (beginning period) and current data for the control and treatment groups and that both are from the same area. One may then compute the percentage difference of the relevant impact variables for the members vis-à-vis the control group. If the percentage change for the treatment group's variable is significantly greater than the comparison group, then that suggests the programme had impact.

In the ideal scenario, with panel data, one can collect the data yearly and compute these differences (Bali Swain and Varghese 2011a). However, panel data also faces limitations when applied to SHGs. First, the SHG programme is already widespread, reaching out to 45 million households, so that one would like to compute the impact of participation for those households from previous loans. Second, panel costs are large and by the time researchers collect and process the data, the programme may have moved on. Third, providing a control group without services for say, one year, is perhaps justifiable, but one cannot deny access and hold a control group for long. The longer the relevant impact measure, the more difficult the task. Certainly so far, no one has collected panel data for SHGs.

As an alternative to panel data, one can proceed in a different direction. So far it has been argued that for a relevant impact study, one would need a control group. Furthermore, ideally one would need to choose the control group with the same external conditions as the treatment group. This selection raises other problems. If one selected both treatment and control group from the same village, for example, then one would wonder why some households chose to participate (or did not choose) to join SHGs. In other words, SHG members may be special. Regression analysis allows one to control any observable differences such as age and gender. With cross-sectional data, however, one cannot control for unobservable differences such as entrepreneurial skill and talent.[5]

Methodology problems

Properly accounting for selection bias entails recognizing that the sample of SHG members may differ from the sample of the population at large. In assessing impact, researchers seek to extricate the causal effect from the potential selection bias.[6] For example, if we observe that income for SHG members has grown over others, is it because of membership or because SHG members are more entrepreneurial? NCAER (2008) may have been motivated by these concerns to measure impact for the same household over time. Unfortunately, NCAER's method creates problems of its own, which are discussed in detail in Bali Swain and Varghese (2011a).

For a scientific impact assessment, one needs a counterfactual so that one can estimate what would have happened if microfinance clients did not receive financial services. Since this is not observable, an appropriate control or comparison group needs to be identified for the treatment group. In experimental designs these are randomly selected from the same population as the treatment group. Randomized studies have led the revolution in the new microeconometrics of development (Banerjee and Duflo 2009). More recently, many researchers have questioned the validity of randomization as the gold standard in impact studies (summarized in Deaton 2010). The data and nature of the SHG programme preclude randomization as a viable option. In their overview on the benefits of randomization, Banerjee and Duflo (2009) carefully discuss when randomized experiments are appropriate. They argue that randomized experiments are particularly strong choices when implemented on a small scale with new interventions. Along with Heckman (1992), they note that the interpretation of randomized experiment becomes inappropriate if one is interested in evaluating the impact of the programme over the population. Bali Swain and Varghese (2011a) argue that as a wide-scale national programme, the SHG programme falls into this category. One could envision a carefully constructed experiment in one village with one programme but an immediate question would arise in its generalizability to other SHG programmes. Randomization also usually studies short-term impact measures but might be difficult to implement for longer-term impact. One cannot hold a control group without training (and/or credit) for long (as noted by Karlan and Goldberg 2006).

Another strategy (as adopted by Pitt and Khandker 1998) exploits an exclusion rule on credit access to estimate unbiased impact. However, SHGs follow no such exogenous rule. Even if such an exclusion rule is applied to a microfinance programme, it is not always a strictly followed eligibility criteria. This might result in empirical evidence that is subject to controversy, as noted by Morduch and Roodman (2009). The inapplicability of randomization and exclusion rules for SHGs leads us to investigate alternative possibilities to evaluate the impact of training for SHG members.

The non-experimental design selects the members of the control/comparison group to match the attributes of the treatment group members as closely as possible. Clients may self-select themselves into participating in the SHG programme resulting in selection bias. Another bias might result from locating the programmes in better or worse-off areas, which might bias the impact due to better or worse level of infrastructure, etc. as compared to a random placement. Meyer (2007) also recounts additional issues in measuring impact correctly. Growth of microfinance supported borrowers may displace the activities of the non-borrowers, and thus needs to be subtracted to measure the gains from microfinance correctly (Bali Swain 2004).

Some researchers have been critical of comparing programmes with a 'no intervention situation' which they term pseudo-counterfactuals. They argue that in the real world policy makers can use resources in several alternative ways. For instance, instead of the resources being used for a microfinance programme they could be utilized for an alternative programme promoting health, education and training skills in women, or supporting them with income generation activities. Thus, to measure the real impact the programme needs to be compared with the counterfactual of the best alternative programme using comparable resources (Ellerman 2007).

Data

The empirical analyses in this book are based on the household survey data which is part of a larger study, the Self Help Group Impact Assessment Survey (SIAS), collected in 2003. SIAS was implemented in two representative districts in each of the five geographically spread states of India. The selected states were Andhra Pradesh and Tamil Nadu in the south, Uttar Pradesh in the north, Orissa in the east and Maharashtra in the west. As of 31 March 2003 the total number of cumulative SHGs in India was around 502,891.[7] Of these 71.32 per cent of the SHGs were concentrated in the southern part of India with almost half (48.5 per cent) of the Indian SHGs in Andhra Pradesh. The eastern and central regions accounted for 9 per cent and 9.6 per cent respectively. Their existence in the northern and western regions was limited to 3.84 per cent and 5.82 per cent respectively. The north-eastern region was a small part of the SBLP with only 0.3 per cent. Given the excessively skewed distribution of SHGs in the south, NABARD has identified 13 poorer states in which they would like to expand their programme. The RBI (2008) also recommends extending the programme to the urban poor.

Instead of a nationally representative sample, the study focuses on the selected districts. Thus, the results of this study are conditional on these states. NABARD's choice to expand the SBLP occurs at the district level without any specific policy to target certain villages (Bali Swain and Varghese 2009). Thus, within the states, the study selected to sample at the district level, which is the basic administrative unit. For the purpose of the survey two representative districts per state were carefully selected. The choice of these two districts was based on the degree of SHGs' exposure (districts with over- and under-exposure to the SBLP were avoided), variety of the SHPIs and good involvement of branches of more than one major bank. Care was also taken that the selected districts captured selected features of the state SHGs. For instance, in Orissa some SHGs were quick to form federations, whereas in Andhra, the majority of groups were promoted by the government. The following districts were selected for the survey: Koraput and Rayagada in Orissa, Medak and Warangal in Andhra Pradesh, Dharmapuri and Villupuram in Tamil Nadu, Allahabad and Rae Bareli in Uttar Pradesh, and Gadchiroli and Chandrapur in Maharashtra (see Figure 2.1). Appendix 1 provides information about the selected districts and the status of the SBLP, based on the interviews of the bank officers, NABARD and government officials, etc.

SIAS comprised of a non-experimental quantitative household survey. A group level survey of the SHGs, where the respondents were office bearers, was also conducted. In addition, a total of 20 focus group discussions (FGD) were conducted to capture the open-ended questions and to understand the needs and get the feedback of the SHG.

The following sampling strategy was used for the household survey. First, SHG member households were randomly chosen in each district. Then, members of the control group were chosen to reflect a comparable socio-economic group as the SHG respondents. These were selected from villages that were similar to the SHG villages in terms of the level of economic development, socio-cultural factors and infra-structural facilities, but did not have a SHG programme (Bali Swain 2003). NABARD's choice to expand the SHG programme occurs at the district level without any specific policy to target certain villages (Bali Swain and Varghese 2009). Thus, we chose to sample at the district level, which is the basic administrative unit within a state.

Due to budget and operational constraints, the sample size was limited to about 1,000 respondents. The process involved discussion with statisticians, economists and practitioners at the stage of sampling design, preparing precoded questionnaires, translation and pilot testing with at least 20 households in each of the five states (100 households in total). The questionnaires were then revised, printed and the data collected by local surveyors who were trained and supervised by the supervisors. The standard checks were applied both in the field and during the data punching process.

The sampling strategy involved random selection of the SHG member-households in each district. The control group (non-SHGs) was chosen to reflect a comparable socio-economic group to the SHG respondents. These households were selected from villages that were similar to the SHG villages in terms of the level of economic development, socio-cultural factors and infrastructure facilities, but did not have a SHG programme. In addition to the 2003 data, recall data for the year 2000 was also collected.

Figure 2.1 Selected states and districts in SIAS survey.

Chapter 5 is the only chapter that uses the data for both the years. For the rest of the analyses, only the 2003 data was used and was further refined. Of the total respondents, a few were from villages with no SHGs. Since these households were not provided the opportunity to self-select, they were dropped. Some old and new SHG respondents were from the same village and this would contaminate the sample since the earlier members may have been different from the later entrants. Of the remaining sample, 604 respondents are from old SHGs, 186 are from new SHGs and 52 are non-members.[8]

At regional (block, district and state) and national level, interviews were conducted with NABARD officers, government agencies and officials, bank managers and NGOs to obtain data about the SHG programme in their local area and to collect information about their experience and approach to SHG promotion. These interviews were based on a semi-structured questionnaires that were prepared to lead the direction and receive feedback.

Data analyses

A characteristic of the SBLP provides us with an opening to properly measure impact. By design, members have to wait to receive a loan from the bank (about six months) and this feature is exploited to identify the self-selected members who have not yet received a loan. In particular, this permits the construction of a counterfactual. In certain districts, some members are currently active members of SHGs. In these same districts (but in other villages), members from newly formed SHGs have been selected but have not yet received financial services. Thus, the control group in our sample consists of the new SHGs, while mature SHGs form the treatment group.[9] It is hypothesized that the old and new SHGs have similar unobservables. Also, the information on the non-members from these districts can be conditioned on the selection to join the SHG. Thus, there are two distinct control groups. The first control group includes SHG members who have not yet received loans while the second includes non-members who have not received loans and are not members.

Raising the level of aggregation to the district level (where both mature and new SHGs reside) the analysis holds the district specific conditions constant. NABARD's choice to expand the SHG programme (at the time of the survey) occurs at the district level without any specific policy that targeted certain villages over others.[10] Thus, unlike other research which uses villages as the aggregation unit, this analysis chooses the districts as the appropriate level of analyses. To account for the remaining village level variability, we employ village level characteristics. It is possible that the district-wide effects may spill over from the mature to the new members and non-members, the estimates would in that case underestimate the impact.

Another critical control is to check whether the old and the new villages differ substantially. This is important since the policy makers might have preferred to expand the SHG programme in certain villages first over others. If infrastructurally better off villages were first chosen for implementing SBLP or if relatively poorer villages were preferred for the programme, it would result in a non-random programme placement bias. In discussions with various officials, and checking of various NABARD and RBI documents, Bali Swain and Varghese (2009) did not find that certain villages were preferred over others at the time of the survey. As an additional check, they checked the observables at various levels of aggregation. A logit regression was estimated for the old and the new SHGs at the village level. They found that none of the village level variables were significant. Similarly, they also checked whether the NGOs favoured certain types of villages earlier than others for linkages? NGOs were found to operate within villages without anticipation of a linkage, i.e. they move independently of the SHG linkage following their own development work.

Ideally, one should also collect data on dropouts to estimate the 'survivorship bias'. However, the dropout rate for SHGs is not severe in that the EDA study estimated the dropout rate as 9.8 per cent, below the 20–30 per cent cited by Armendáriz and Morduch and Karlan as a severe problem.[11] Furthermore, the EDA study indicates that almost 50 per cent of the SHGs had no dropouts, and one-third had two or fewer dropouts. The very poor had a higher dropout rate of 11 per cent but not considerably higher than the 7 per cent of the non-poor. A more systematic analysis by Baland *et al.* (2008) also did not find much attrition in SHG groups but noted that those who did drop out were more socially disadvantaged. The dropouts were not traced in the SIAS household survey but, considering the slightly higher dropout rate of the very poor in SHG programmes, the estimates presented here might slightly overestimate the impact. Thus, the results of this study are conditional on the remaining mature SHG members being similar to the dropouts.

Impact assessment methodologies used

Coleman's pipeline method

Coleman (1999) proposed the pipeline approach, where he compares current members to future members who have not yet received loans. Bali Swain and Varghese (2009, 2010) show how Coleman's approach may be adapted to the SBLP framework to measure the impact. While Coleman surveyed borrowers in both treatment and control villages, they observe new and mature groups in SHGs in different villages but in the same district.[12] The SHG members have to wait to receive a loan from the bank (about six months). Bali Swain and Varghese use this feature to identify the self-selected members who have not yet received a loan. Their technique differs from Coleman's as he interviewed people at the data design stage while they exploit the initial waiting period that some households have to face in obtaining loans from later SHGs.

Bali Swain and Varghese (2009) make the following adaptations to suggest that the critical variable to test is SHGMON, or the number of months since a member has joined a SHG. Since an SHG is bank linked only six months after formation, we needed to take those six months into account. Almost all the new SHG respondents in SIAS data had been members for less than six months and for these SHGMON=0. Only 14 of these new respondents were members for more than six months, in which case we subtract six months from the date of formation. Similarly, for the mature SHGs, their SHGMON was calculated by subtracting six months from their membership. A few mature SHG respondents did not report the date of their SHG formation.[13]

Keeping in mind the outlined procedure and data, the following regression is estimated:

$$I_{ijs} = a + \alpha X_{ijs} + \beta V_{js} + \lambda Ds + \gamma M_{ijs} + \delta \text{SGHMON}_{ijs} + \eta ijs \qquad (2.1)$$

where I_{ijs} is the impact for household measured in terms of asset accumulation or income generation, for household i in village j and district s, X_{ijs} are the household characteristics; V_{js} is a vector of village level characteristics, and Ds is a vector of district dummies that control for any district level difference. Here, M_{ijs} is the membership dummy variable, which controls for the selection bias; it takes the value 1 for both mature and new SHGs, and the value 0 for those villagers that have chosen not to access the programme. Here, SGHMON_{ijs} is the number of months that SHG credit was available to mature members, which is exogenous to the households.

Propensity score matching

Another methodology to correct for selection bias created by programme selection, is the propensity score matching (PSM) method.[14] This technique allows the identification of the programme impact when a random experiment is not implemented, as long as there is a counterfactual or control group. In contrast to other regression methods, the PSM does not depend on linearity and has a weaker assumption on the error term. The matching relies on the assumption of conditional independence of potential outcomes and treatment given observables. The SIAS household survey data collection method meets these three conditions outlined in Heckman *et al.* (1997), thus allowing the use of the PSM method. First, the survey questionnaire is the same for participants and non-participants and therefore yields the same outcome measures. Second, both groups come from the same local environment or markets. Third, a rich set of observables for both outcome and participation variables are available for the performance of the PSM method.

As with any impact evaluation, the main problem with identifying SBLP impact is that the outcome indicator for SHG member households with and without programme is not observed because, by definition, all the participants are SHG members in the first period. Since one can only have information on the households once they participate in the programme, there is a need to identify a control group that allows us to infer what would have happened with the SHG participant household if the SBLP had not been implemented. The PSM uses the "propensity score" or the conditional probability of participation to identify a counterfactual group of non-participants, given conditional independence.

The probability ($P(X)$) of being selected is first determined by a logit equation and then this probability (the propensity score) is used to match the households. Y_1 is the outcome indicator for the SHG programme participants ($T=1$), and Y_0 is the outcome indicator for the SHG members ($T=0$), then equation (2.2) denotes the mean impact:

$$\Delta = E\left[Y_1 \mid T = 1, P(X)\right] - E\left[Y_0 \mid T = 0, P(X)\right] \qquad (2.2)$$

where the propensity score matching estimator is the mean difference in the outcomes over common support, weighted by the propensity score distribution of participants. The impact may now be estimated on our outcome variables taking the selection bias from participation into account. Heckman *et al.* (1997) suggest that in small samples the choice of the matching algorithm can be important, due to trade-offs between bias and variances. Thus, Caliendo and Kopeinig (2008) suggest that multiple algorithms should be tried and if they give similar results, the choice may be unimportant.

The literature proposes several propensity score matching methods to identify a comparison group.[15] Since the probability of two households being exactly matched is close to zero, distance measures are used to match households. Using two different algorithms for propensity score matching to identify the comparison group, the average treatment effect on treated (ATT) is measured by the nearest neighbour matching algorithm

(NN) and the local linear regression. The NN is the more intuitive of the two as it matches each treated observation to a control observation with the closest propensity score. The local linear regression (LLR) method[16] uses the weighted average of nearly all individuals in the control group to construct the counterfactual outcome. Bootstrapped standard errors for the LLR procedures are used in the reported results (Abadie and Imbens 2007; Heckman *et al.* 1997). The ATT estimates of SHG participation are then estimated for the relevant outcome variable.

Testing for robustness of results with sensitivity analysis

The propensity score matching hinges on the conditional independence or unconfoundedness assumption (CIA) and unobserved variables that affect the participation and the outcome variable simultaneously that may lead to a hidden bias due to which the matching estimators may not be robust. However, it is not possible to directly reject the unconfoundedness assumption. Heckman and Hotz (1989) and Rosenbaum (1987) have developed indirect ways of assessing this assumption. These methods rely on estimating a causal effect that is known to be equal to zero. If the test suggests that this causal effect differs from zero, the unconfoundedness assumption is considered less plausible (Imbens 2004).

Building on Rosenbaum and Rubin (1983) and Rosenbaum (1987), Ichino *et al.* (2007) propose a sensitivity analysis that has been employed in Chapters 3 and 6 of this book. They suggest that if the CIA is not satisfied given observables but is satisfied if one could observe an additional binary variable (confounder), then this potential confounder could be simulated in the data and used as an additional covariate in combination with the preferred matching estimator. The comparison of the estimates obtained with and without matching on the simulated confounder shows to what extent the baseline results are robust to specific sources of failure of the CIA, since the distribution of the simulated variable can be constructed to capture different hypotheses on the nature of potential confounding factors.

In Chapter 6 the pipeline method is combined with other propensity score matching methods. While investigating the impact of SBLP training programmes, one faces a double selection problem. At one level it is the issue of self-selection into membership and, on the other hand, the members make the decision to undertake training or not. Ideally one would need to turn to non-experimental methods but due to reasons specified earlier, alternative methodologies may be employed.

PSM methods are used to predict (either through a logit or probit equation) who will decide to train, and generate a propensity score or a probability of choosing to train. Those who would choose training are then matched with those who decide not to train and any differential between the treatment and control groups is attributed to training. The Coleman methodology is used to account for the member selection. The combination of these methods is referred to as regression adjusted matching. These methods may be implemented directly with readily available software programmes (see Ichino and Becker 2002; Leuven and Sianesi 2009).

Additional methodological issues

Two other challenging issues are those of estimating women empowerment and vulnerability.[17] The methodologies to estimate both these concepts are briefly introduced here. Chapter 3 discusses the strategy to estimate vulnerability in greater detail, while women empowerment is discussed extensively in Chapter 5.

Apart from conceptually being a complex issue, women empowerment is a latent variable and cannot be measured directly. An effort to measure empowerment, such as using a composite index, suffers from the arbitrary assignment of weights to variables. An additional difficulty is that many of the variables are ordinal in nature and assigning a numerical value may be inappropriate. One possibility is to follow Bali Swain and Wallentin (2009) in employing Jöreskog's LISREL structural modelling method in which the unobserved univariate continuous distribution generates an observed ordinal distribution as a latent response distribution (Jöreskog 2002). The underlying variable therefore assigns a metric to the ordinal variable. In contrast to the pipeline method used in other chapters for measuring impact, Chapter 5 divides the households into SHG members and control group and employs structural equation for analysing the change in women's empowerment between 2000 and 2003.

3 Reducing poverty and vulnerability[1]

Introduction

Vulnerability, as recognized in a number of studies, remains a critical issue among rural low income households, especially in precipitation dependent areas where the effects of shocks are likely to be substantial and even dramatic (Dercon 2005; World Bank 2000). Dercon (2005) points out that these shocks can take 'on a variety of forms but many can lead to substantial loss of income, wealth or consumption' (p. 5). He also asserts that 'the inability to smooth consumption has implications for poverty in a direct way: households may drift occasionally under some socially acceptable level, possibly bounce back up and drift back in' (pp. 6, 10).

The threat of loss of or decline in farm earnings of the rural poor may be brought about by environmental conditions that affect their output. Natural catastrophes like drought, floods, pests, etc. and market fluctuations may lead to changes in input and product prices. Yield risks are especially significant when agricultural price and other supports are inadequate or non-existent. There are other types of risk as well, induced by the possibility of income decline in non-farm activities. In addition, unexpected shocks due to illness, death, etc. are anticipated given the health related environment and poor medical services they generally face. This variety of risks translates into serious concerns regarding food security, ability to buy inputs, to pay school fees for children, seek medical help when ill, maintain tools or equipment, to work, to repay loans, etc. Vulnerability therefore relates to the claims or rights over resources in dealing with risks, shocks and economic stresses.

An extensive literature has investigated the impact of microfinance in alleviating poverty and several studies have shown positive impact in reducing poverty (Morduch 1999). But a growing number of researchers have challenged this view, emphasizing that the results are more mixed (Amin *et al.* 1999; Puhazhendi and Badatya 2002; Armendáriz and

Morduch 2005; Karlan 2007).[2] Hence, analysing beyond poverty, this chapter investigates if the SBLP reduces household vulnerability. In other words, does SBLP reduce the household exposure to future shocks and improve their ability to cope with them? Examining this question is critical since the objective of poverty alleviation is not just obtaining increased economic welfare through increased incomes and consumption. It is also about creating ways to prevent households from falling into poverty and enabling them to meet their survival needs including food security, to make productive investments and create assets to positively impact their economic status in the long term. Faced by economic hardships many poor households dissolve their assets. Thus alleviating poverty should also ensure that the poor avoid selling their limited resources in times of income or expenditure shocks. While static poverty measures are helpful in assessing the current poverty status of households they tend to ignore poverty dynamics over time.[3] Households that do not fall below the poverty line are not officially considered poor and thus lie outside the purview of various poverty alleviation programmes. But their degree of vulnerability or the risk of their being poor in the future may still remain very high. The cumulative impact of SBLP on the household's well-being may therefore not be captured by standard poverty measures alone. A limited literature on the impact of microfinance on vulnerability provides evidence that microfinance tends to strengthen crisis coping mechanisms, helps diversify income-earning sources and enables asset creation. In fact, a few studies suggest that it has a more significant impact in reducing vulnerability than income-poverty (Hashemi *et al.* 1996; Morduch 1999).

Two important dimensions of well-being, namely, poverty and *ex-ante* vulnerability of households in SHG and non-SHG groups, are estimated in this chapter. It further investigates whether microfinance programmes like the Self Help Group programme (SBLP) lead to a reduction in vulnerability or not. Bali Swain and Floro (2012) defines vulnerability as a forward-looking, *ex-ante* measure of the household's ability to cope with future shocks and proneness to food insecurity that can undermine the household's survival and the development of its members' capabilities. SBLP impact may also be heterogeneous depending on the level of village infrastructure development, which may translate microfinance delivery into better outcomes. For instance, lack of (or distance from) paved roads negatively impacts communication, connectivity and market access and hence may undermine the impact of SHG participation on vulnerability and food expenditure. Thus, the impact of SBLP on vulnerability might vary with respect to infrastructural development level of the participant's village and the linkage model that is used to deliver microfinance (Bali Swain 2012).

Based on the empirical analysis of the household level data from the Self Help Group Impact Assessment Survey (SIAS), various poverty measures are estimated. An *ex-ante* vulnerability measure using Chauduri *et al.* (2002) methodology is also estimated to gauge the extent of SBLP impact on poverty. This permits the estimation of the magnitude of the household vulnerability estimation using cross-sectional data. Taking into account the variation in the effect of SHG participation on vulnerability due to difference in the economic environment and the design of the SHG bank linkage, potential selection bias is corrected for, using propensity score matching to obtain the average treatment on treated effect (impact) on vulnerability. Finally the sensitivity of the results to unobservables is tested.

Understanding poverty and vulnerability

While poverty is defined in a number of ways, it is increasingly evident that an *ex-ante* assessment of vulnerability provides crucial information about households' well-being that a static, *ex-post* assessment of current poverty does not (Carter and Barrett 2006; Calvo and Dercon 2005; Kamanou and Morduch 2005). Vulnerability takes into account the fact that households face a multitude of risks, and those that have little resources to fall back upon end up making decisions that help them mitigate or manage risks or cope with shocks. Calvo and Dercon (2005) point out that poverty measurement involving the choice of a welfare indicator, the identification of the 'poor' via some norm (for instance, the poverty line) and an aggregation procedure tend to take place in a world of certainty. However, in the real world the quality of life may deteriorate and persons' capabilities become at risk not only due to current shortfalls in harvests, earnings, food, funds for schooling, etc., but also due to the distress caused by insecurity and powerlessness in the face of future shortfalls. They argue that vulnerability to poverty in any dimension (consumption, health and so forth) is a form of hardship in itself. Kamanou and Morduch (2005) further point out that vulnerability also applies to poor households in that they face the risk of changing their poverty status from, for example, poor to severe poverty.

Vulnerability has been interpreted by researchers in different ways, thus leading to several definitions and measures. Bali Swain and Floro (2012) discuss a few prominent notions of vulnerability that are presented in this section. Some see vulnerability as a condition which can cause poverty or constrain people from escaping out of poverty (Prowse 2003). The view that poor people are generally more vulnerable is shared by Cannon *et al.* (2003) and Feldbrügge and von Braun (2002). Other researchers have taken a different view of vulnerability. They identify poverty as one element, which may contribute to an enhanced vulnerability (Cardona 2004). Still others, such as Calvo (2008), treat vulnerability as a dimension of poverty, where vulnerability is defined as a threat of suffering any form of poverty in the future.[4] Calvo and Dercon (2005) view vulnerability as a combination of poverty and risk. Poverty is seen as the failure to reach a minimum outcome, whereas risk is measured as the distribution over different states of the world that translate into a threat of being poor in the next period. This idea of vulnerability builds upon the probability of outcomes failing to reach the minimal standard threshold and the uncertainty about how far households may fall below that threshold. This uncertainty is a source of distress and has a direct detrimental impact on the household's well-being.

Chauduri *et al.* (2002) define vulnerability within the framework of poverty eradication as the *ex-ante* risk that a household will, if currently non-poor, fall below the poverty line, or if currently poor, will remain in poverty. It is based on the notion of vulnerability as the probability of being poor and implies accounting for the expected (mean) consumption, as well as the volatility (variance) of its future consumption stream. The stochastic process generating the consumption of the household is dependent on the household characteristics and the error term (with mean zero). It captures the idiosyncratic shocks to consumption that are identically and independently distributed over time for each household. Hence, any unobservable sources of persistent or serially correlated shocks or unobserved household specific effects over time on household consumption are ruled out. It also assumes economic stability, thereby ruling out the possibility of aggregate shocks. Thus the future consumption shocks are assumed to be idiosyncratic in nature. This does not mean, however, that they are identically distributed across households. Furthermore, it is assumed that the variance of the idiosyncratic factors (shocks) depends upon observable household characteristics.

Ligon and Schechter (2003) take a utilitarian approach to define vulnerability, arguing that it depends not only on the mean of household consumption but also on the variation in consumption in the context of a risky environment. They decompose the risk faced by the household into aggregate and idiosyncratic risk.

A growing number of empirical studies have proposed varied measures and proxy indicators of vulnerability as well (Zimmerman and Carter 2003; Calvo and Dercon 2005; Glewwe and Hall 1998; Ligon and Schechter 2003; Carter and Barrett 2006; Morduch 2004). When available some empirical studies use household panel data, to analyse the extent of consumption variation over time as households experience income fluctuations (Morduch 2004; Kamanou and Morduch 2005). Other studies examine the impact of various forms of shocks on households' consumption (Ligon and Schechter 2003; Carter *et al.* 2007), or other aspects of household well-being, for instance, health (Dercon and Hoddinott 2005). However, empirical analyses of vulnerability remain severely constrained due the paucity of panel data in several developing countries. Attempts are being made to address these data constraints but there is limited information on the idiosyncratic and covariate shocks experienced by households (Günther and Harttgen 2009). In this chapter the impact on vulnerability is estimated using the Chauduri *et al.* (2002) methodology. It allows the estimation of vulnerability using cross-sectional household data, thereby enabling the estimation of vulnerability using the SIAS survey. The Chauduri *et al.* vulnerability measure has been adopted in a number of vulnerability studies including Zhang and Wan (2006), Günther and Harttgen (2009) and Imai *et al.* (2010)[5] and is considered to be one of the best estimators. In a comparative study of various vulnerability estimation strategies, Ligon and Schechter (2004) find that when the environment is stationary and consumption expenditures are measured without error, then the estimator proposed by Chauduri *et al.* is the best estimator of vulnerability.

SHG household poverty and vulnerability

Only a few studies have explored the impact of microfinance in terms of reducing vulnerability. Evidence on Bangladeshi microfinance institutions conclude that microfinance access has led to consumption smoothing or a reduction in the variance in consumption by member households across time periods (Khandker 1998; Morduch 1999). Puhazhendi and Badatya's (2002) study on SBLP finds that microfinance provides loans for both production and consumption purposes, thereby allowing consumption smoothing and enabling households to mitigate the effects of negative shocks.

Studying SHG members in the southern state of Tamil Nadu over a period of five years, Guérin *et al.* (2009) find that the proportion of financially secure families increased and doubled between 2004 and 2009. However, the number of highly insecure families in 2004 were half as many as those in 2009. The main reason for the inability of the poor families to come out of poverty were the social emergency expenditures related to birth, death or religious functions. Major health shocks to the family that required prolonged and expensive treatment were another reason. About the same proportion of the households improved their situation as those that were worse off, thus the results of the impact of SHG linkage was not conclusive from this study.

Bali Swain and Floro (2007) argue that SHG participation can help member households facing liquidity constraints and multiple risks, thereby reducing their vulnerability. The members of SHGs may share each other's risk through institutionalized arrangements, by lending to members who face liquidity constraints in meeting investment needs or in meeting unexpected consumption expenses. Such production and consumption loans strengthen the members' productivity and earnings and help their household's ability to cope with contingencies and idiosyncratic shocks. Additional training provided to members by the SHG programme also helps enhance the entrepreneurship skills as well as their capacity to use information, evaluate and adjust to changes, thus increasing both their productivity and self-confidence.

In addition to the pecuniary effect of production loan provisioning, SHGs may promote or strengthen social networks that provide mutual support by facilitating the pooling of savings, regular meetings, etc. that help empower their members, especially women. Group meetings are often used to discuss various personal, social and economic issues leading to improved ability of the member households to manage risk and deal with shocks. Bali Swain and Floro (2007) further argue that the non-pecuniary effects of SHG participation can reduce the vulnerability of the members and by their households in more ways than those that are captured by the change in the household earnings.

Though SHGs may be capable of dealing with vulnerability to idiosyncratic shocks they might not be as effective when faced with covariate shocks such as epidemics, flooding or declining crop prices (Zimmerman and Carter 2003; Morduch 2004; Dercon 2005). Rural livelihoods in developing countries like India often exhibit high correlations between risks faced by households in the same village or area. Hence when farm prices decline, or there is a drought or flood in the area, all households are adversely affected simultaneously. Group-based systems, such as SBLP, may be weak and/or ineffective in the situation of such 'covariate' shocks.[6] Thus while SHGs can be of help in cases when a household faces an idiosyncratic shock, the protection afforded by SHG in dealing with aggregate shocks is likely to be limited. An enabling economic environment and the presence of additional services and infrastructural support such as health centres and flood control systems will be crucial to reducing exposure to these aggregate shocks and enhance the effectiveness of SHGs in reducing household vulnerability.

Estimating poverty and vulnerability

The characteristics of the SHG and non-SHG members and their households are presented in Table 3.1 (Bali Swain and Floro 2012). In general,

Table 3.1 Selected characteristics of survey respondents and their households (standard deviation in parentheses)

	All	SHG members	Non-SHG[††]
N	840	789	51
Average real food expenditure per capita per month	307 (442)	308 (453)	282 (194)
Average age of respondent	35 (8.41)	35 (8.44)	36 (8.08)
Proportion with some (in %)			
Primary education	18	18	24 (0.43)
Secondary education	17	18	12
Post-secondary education	3	3	2
Average number of children	1.5 (1.27)	1.5 (1.27)	1.4 (1.25)
Dependency ratio	0.66 (0.22)	0.66 (0.22)	0.62 (0.23)
Average number of workers in the household	2.48 (1.24)	2.46 (1.23)	2.70 (1.40)
Average number of workers engaged in primary activity	2.49 (1.37)	2.48 (1.37)	2.55 (1.30)
Mean size of owned land in 2000 (in acres)	0.85 (1.43)	0.87 (1.45)	0.48** (1.12)
Mean value of non-land wealth in 2000 (in rupees)[†]	64,691 (90197)	63,708 (86775)	79,891 (132625)
Distance to bank (in km)	7.33 (6.87)	7.48 (7.02)	4.96***(3.16)
Distance to healthcare	3.55 (2.84)	3.46 (2.78)	4.95*** (3.30)
Distance to market	5.39 (4.02)	5.38 (4.07)	5.46 (3.16)
Distance to paved road	3.06 (3.32)	3.03 (3.33)	3.59 (3.04)
Distance to bus stop	3.75 (3.55)	3.69 (3.59)	4.71** (2.76)
Lack of cash or food in 2000	0.38 (0.49)	0.39 (0.49)	0.27* (0.45)

Source: Bali Swain and Floro 2012, p. 23.

Notes

† Calculated with 2000 as the base year. †† *t*-test results for equality of means of SHG members and non-SHG members are indicated by *** if significant at 1% level, ** if significant at 5% level, and * if significant at 10% level.

SHG members are younger but have a higher level of education. On average member households have a lower non-land wealth as compared to the non-SHG respondents. They also have higher food consumption per capita per month and hold larger landholdings relative to non-SHG households. However, there is a large variation in the quality of these landholdings. Typically, SHG households live in villages that are closer to public transport and primary healthcare centres but further away from banks, compared to non-SHG households. Using a subjective indicator based on the survey response as to whether or not the respondent household experienced severe shortage of food and/or cash in the past three years, about 39 per cent of the SHG respondents reported experiencing economic difficulties as compared to 27 per cent of non-SHG households. The *t*-test results confirms the difference between the SHG members and non-members in terms of size of landholdings and their access to market infrastructure and services. The incidence of food and/or cash shortage in the past is also found to be statistically significant.

The SBLP has been promoted as an important poverty alleviation strategy in India, with the intention of reducing poverty and promoting economic and social empowerment of the participating households. Given the non-experimental nature of the SIAS data, before estimating poverty and vulnerability, propensity score matching (PSM) is employed to correct for selection bias. As explained in Chapter 2, this technique enables the identification of the programme impact when a random experiment is not implemented, using a counterfactual or control group. In contrast to other regression methods, the PSM does not depend on linearity and has a weaker assumption on the error term. The PSM uses the propensity score or the conditional probability of participation to identify a counterfactual group of non-participants, given conditional independence. The probability of being selected is determined by a logit equation and then this probability (the propensity score) is used to match similar households. Once the households have been matched to rectify the selection bias the poverty profile of the matched sample is constructed.

The poverty profile of the SHG and non-SHG households is examined using standard measures of poverty such as the headcount ratio, poverty gap ratio and the squared poverty gap or Foster–Greer–Thorbecke (FGT) index. The headcount ratio measures the proportion of population under the poverty line. The depth of poverty is measured by the poverty gap ratio, which is the total amount that is needed to raise the poor from their present incomes to the poverty line as a proportion of the poverty line and averaged over the total population. The severity of poverty is captured by the squared poverty gap or FGT index that takes inequality among the poor into account.

The poverty line used in estimating the above indices is based on the official (consumption-based) poverty line for India, which assumes the minimum subsistence requirement of 2,400 calories per capita per day for rural areas. The official poverty line estimate is derived from the household consumer expenditure data collected by National Sample Survey Organization (NSSO) of the Ministry of Statistics and Programme Implementation every fifth year. To match the data the poverty line estimate is drawn from the 61st round of the NSS which covers the period July 2004 to June 2005.[7] Following Bali Swain and Floro (2012) it is then adjusted to the official poverty line using the 2003 Consumer Price Index for agricultural workers in rural areas to correspond with the survey period. Hence the estimated 2003 poverty line is Rs.356.3 per capita per month.

Bali Swain and Floro (2012) estimate the household's vulnerability using the Chauduri, Jayan and Suryahadi (2002) approach that allows the estimation of expected consumption and its variance with cross-section data. Following them, it is assumed that the vulnerability level of a household h at time t is defined as the probability that the household finds itself to be consumption poor in period $t+1$. The household's consumption level is deemed to be dependent upon several factors such as wealth, current income, expectation of future income (i.e. lifetime prospects), the uncertainty it faces regarding its future income and its ability to smooth consumption in the face of various income shocks. Each of these, in turn, depends on a number of household characteristics, both observed and unobserved, the socio-economic environment in which the household is situated, and the shocks that contribute to differential welfare outcomes for households that are otherwise observationally equivalent. Hence, the household's vulnerability level in terms of its future food consumption can be expressed as a reduced form for consumption determined by a set of variables X_{ht}:

$$\ln c_{ht} = \beta_0 + X_{ht}\beta_1 + \mu_{ht} \tag{3.1}$$

Where $\ln c_{ht}$ represents log of consumption per capita on adult equivalence scale, X_{ht} represents selected household and community level characteristics, and μ_{ht} is the unexplained part of household consumption. Since the impact of shocks on household consumption is correlated with the observed characteristics, the variance of the unexplained part of consumption μ_{ht} is:

$$\sigma_h^2 = \Phi_0 + \Phi_1 X_{ht} + \omega_{ht} \tag{3.2}$$

which implies that the variance of the error term is not equal across households and depends upon X_{hi}. The latter includes respondent's educational attainment, household composition, number of workers in the household and household wealth proxy. The environment characteristics such as access to paved roads, markets, healthcare services, and public transportation are also taken into account. Given data limitations, one cannot identify the particular stochastic process generating β. The expected mean and variance per capita household food consumption are estimated using a simple functional form by Amemiya's (1977) three-step feasible generalized least squares (FGLS).[8] Using the obtained β_1 and Φ_1 estimates, the expected log consumption and the variance of log consumption for each household is then estimated. These serve as vulnerability estimates.

To facilitate comparison of the vulnerability distribution among SHG and non-SHG households, additional measures using different thresholds are estimated. This is done in order to examine the sensitivity of the vulnerability results to the choice of vulnerability threshold. The relative vulnerability threshold uses the observed poverty rate in the population, which is approximately equal to the mean vulnerability level within a group in the absence of aggregate shocks (Chauduri *et al.* 2002). Thus, vulnerability levels above the observed poverty rate threshold imply that the household's risk of poverty is greater than the average risk in the population, thus making it more vulnerable. The official rural poverty rate by the Planning Commission of India is used to estimate this vulnerability threshold.[9]

Another vulnerability threshold that is used is 0.50. Following Chauduri *et al.* (2002), the households with vulnerability levels between observed poverty rates and 0.50 threshold are termed relatively vulnerable whereas those above 0.50 are considered highly vulnerable. Finally, the vulnerability to poverty ratio that measures the fraction of the vulnerable population to the fraction that is poor is also estimated. The higher the vulnerability to poverty ratio the more spread is the distribution of vulnerability, whereas a lower vulnerability to poverty ratio implies greater concentration of vulnerability amongst a few households. Admittedly, the selection of the vulnerability thresholds is arbitrary in nature, thus it becomes important to compare the vulnerability estimates using additional vulnerability thresholds to test the sensitivity of the results to the choice of vulnerability threshold.

To measure the impact of SBLP on vulnerability, the mean difference in the outcomes over common support, weighted by the propensity score distribution of the participants is estimated, using the propensity score matching estimator as discussed earlier in Chapter 2.

Poverty and vulnerability profile for SHG and non-SHG members

The empirical evidence presented in this section is based on Bali Swain and Floro (2012). The poverty profiles of the SHGs (treatment group) and the non-SHG members (control group) are constructed using standard measures such as the headcount index, poverty gap index and the squared poverty gap index.[10] These are presented in Table 3.2, which gives the poverty profile of the SHG member and non-member households using standard poverty measures.[11] The results show that a higher proportion of the SHG members are poor (72.5 per cent as compared to 60.8 per cent for the non-members) although the depth of poverty is about the same between SHG and non-SHG households. The aggregate poverty gap per SHG member household is about Rs.123, as compared to Rs.118 among the non-SHGs member households. The FGT index further shows that there is slightly greater inequality among the non-SHG poor (0.24) vis-à-vis than the SHG poor (0.22).

The mean vulnerability level within the SHG member-household group is much lower (0.45) and statistically significant as compared to the SHG non-members (0.62). This implies that participation in SHGs may reduce

Table 3.2 Poverty and vulnerability estimates for SHG members and non-SHG members[†] (standard deviation in parentheses)

	SHG members	Non-SHG members[††]
All Households		
N	691	51
Poverty Profile for SHG members and non-members		
Headcount ratio (per cent)	72.5	60.8
Aggregate poverty gap per observation	123	118
Poverty gap ratio (per cent)	35	34
Foster-Greer-Thorbecke (squared poverty gap)	0.22	0.24
Vulnerability Profile for SHG members and non-members		
Mean	0.45 (0.39)	0.62***(0.39)
Fraction vulnerability	0.55	0.72**
Fraction relatively vulnerable	0.08	0.03
Fraction highly vulnerable	0.47	0.69**
Vulnerability to poverty ratio	0.75	1.18

Source: Bali Swain and Floro 2012.

Notes
† The vulnerability estimates are based on the Chauduri *et al.* (2002) method.
†† *t*-test results for equality of means and proportion.
***, ** and * indicate significance at 10%, 5% and 1% levels respectively.

the vulnerability of the households. Examining the mean vulnerability and sensitivity of the vulnerability estimate to the choice of a threshold three different vulnerability thresholds are presented in Table 3.2, namely: 1) the observed poverty rate; 2) the vulnerability threshold of lying above the observed poverty rate but with a 50 per cent probability of falling into poverty at least once in the next year; and 3) the highly vulnerable lying above the vulnerability threshold of 0.5 for a one year time period. The ratio of the proportion of households that are vulnerable to the proportion that are poor are also reported. This is an indication of how dispersed vulnerability is in the population.

Even though a higher proportion of SHG members are poor, they are relatively less vulnerable (0.55) as compared to the non-SHG (0.72). Not only are the non-SHG members more vulnerable, a larger proportion of them (0.69) exhibit a high degree of vulnerability. The non-members also have a higher vulnerability to poverty ratio (1.18) with a greater dispersion in incidence of vulnerability.

These results indicate that there is a large proportion of currently poor SHG members, with vulnerability levels low enough for them to be classified as non-vulnerable. This reflects the stochastic nature of the relationship between poverty and vulnerability. Even though poverty and vulnerability are related concepts, the characteristics of those in poverty at any given point in time may differ from the characteristics of those who are vulnerable to poverty.

The ATT point estimates that measure the mean impact of SBLP on vulnerability are presented for all SHGs and mature SHGs in Table 3.3. Column (1) shows that the ATT point estimates (both neighbour to

Table 3.3 Average treatment on treated estimates of SHG participation impact on vulnerability and average food expenditure per capita per month

Matching algorithm	(1) Vulnerability	(2) Average food expenditure per capita per month
All SHG members		
1NN	0.09 (1.19)	29.04 (0.61)
LLR (bw 1)	0.11 (1.54)	68.35* (1.89)
Mature SHG members		
1NN	−0.15** (0.73)	39.33 (42.31)
LLR (bw1)	−0.11* (0.61)	66.80 (42.55)

Source: Bali Swain and Floro 2012.

Notes
** Significant at the 5% level. * Significant at the 10% level. NN=neighbour to neighbour, *t*-statistics in parentheses. LLR=local linear regression, *p*-values in parentheses standard errors created by bootstrap replications of 200.

neighbour (NN) and local linear regression (LLR)) are positive but statistically insignificant for vulnerability. This reveals that after accounting for the selection bias the SHG members are neither more nor less vulnerable as compared to the non-members. However, the SHG participants that have been members for over a year show a significantly lower level of vulnerability. This indicates that it takes some time before the impact of participation in microfinance is observed on vulnerability. By design, the SHG–Bank Linkage Programme provides credit to those groups that have demonstrated financial maturity and stability during the first six months of their existence. Thus, not only are the more mature (older than one year) groups credit linked they also have higher saving funds that may be used for intra-group lending to the members. This provides them with a greater possibility to use microfinance for reducing vulnerability, unlike the newly formed SHGs. SBLP participation on the other hand does lead to an increase in the member's average food expenditure per capita per month compared to that of the non-SHGs, using the LLR algorithm method (Table 3.3, column (2)). A likely reason for this might be due to the provisioning of SHG loans that may be used for any purpose (including consumption) and thus help the households cope with economic shocks. Taking the subset of the more mature SHGs, however, the results do not show any significant increase in average food expenditure. Bali Swain and Floro (2012) argue that these results show that even though the current poverty status of SHG member households has a very high proportion of poor with a higher aggregate poverty gap, their propensity to become poor in the next period (vulnerability) is not higher. In fact, the more mature SHG participants have a significantly lower level of vulnerability.

To check the robustness of these ATT estimates, Bali Swain and Floro (2012) perform sensitivity analysis. They use two covariates to simulate the confounder, namely: young (respondents under the age of 26 years) and illiterate (with no education). These covariates are selected in order to capture the effect of 'unobservables' like ability, entrepreneurial skills, experience and risk aversion. These may have an impact on the member participation in the SHG programme and on the vulnerability of the household. If the ATT estimate changes dramatically with respect to the confounders, then it would imply that the results are not robust. The Kernel matching algorithm with between-imputation standard error is employed in order to use only the variability of the simulated ATT across iterations. The results of these two confounders[12] 'young' and 'no education' are very close to the baseline estimate. They find that the outcome and the selection effect on vulnerability is positive but not very large. The results indicate a robustness of the matching estimates.

Vulnerability and delivery mechanism[13]

As discussed in Chapter 1, the SBLP links the SHGs with the banks through Self Help Promoting Institutions (SHPIs). Three types of linkages have emerged as the most common. In linkage model 1, banks both form and finance the SHGs. In the most popular linkage model 2 (roughly three-quarters of all SHGs), NGOs and other agencies form the groups but banks directly finance them. In the third linkage model, banks finance the SHGs through NGOs.

The effectiveness of credit delivery can play a crucial role in enhancing the impact of any programme on reducing vulnerability. The researchers and practitioners have been anxious to know if better infrastructure like paved roads support greater impact of SHG through improved access to markets and faster communication and transportation. Further, the effectiveness of credit delivery through various linkage models has also been much debated by practitioners and researchers. Using the SIAS data these issues have been further investigated by Bali Swain (2012). These results are presented in this section. Table 3.4 shows that the SHG members are poorer with a headcount ratio of 78.8 per cent (67.8 per cent) as compared to 66.7 per cent (58.3 per cent) of the non-SHG members in the villages that are less than one kilometre from the paved roads (greater than one kilometre from the paved roads). The intensity of poverty appears to be the highest for the non-SHG members in the villages that are closer to the paved roads (as reflected in the aggregate poverty gap of Rs.139.5, poverty gap ratio of 40 and squared poverty gap of 0.27). The SHGs that have been formed and financed by the banks (model 1) have the highest proportion of poor (81.4 per cent), whereas those belonging to NGOs formed SHGs (models 2 and 3) tend to have lower poverty rates (70.6 per cent and 74 per cent respectively).

The most popular linkage model 2 (NGO formed but directly financed by banks) SHGs have relatively lower proportion of poor and are better-off in terms of the poverty gap and severity. Infrastructure (as proxied by distance from the paved road) has a definitive larger impact on reduction of vulnerability. SHG members show a greater reduction in their vulnerability (vis-à-vis the non-SHG members) for villages with better infrastructure (see Table 3.5), indicating that greater infrastructural development enables SHGs to amplify their impact on vulnerability reduction.

The SHPI that links the SHGs to the banks may have a significant impact on credit delivery. With NGOs, government and bankers getting involved with the SHGs there have been growing concerns about the quality of SBLP credit delivery. Investigating further by the type of linkage, Table 3.6 shows that SHG participation has a strong significant impact on reducing vulnerability if the NGOs specialize in training and banks in lending (the more popular linkage model 2). Bali Swain (2012) checks for the robustness of these results using Rosenbaum (2002). This approach determines how strongly an unmeasured variable influences the selection process to undermine the implication of the matching analyses. The bounds for the average treatment effects on the treated are estimated in the presence of unobserved heterogeneity (hidden bias) between treatment and control cases. The results show that the unobserved effect would have to increase the odds of participation in SHG by more than double before one changes the conclusions about the effect of SHG participation on participants. Thus, the postulated positive impact of the SHG participation on mean vulnerability is a robust result according to this test.

Concluding discussion

In this chapter we investigated the SBLP impact on vulnerability, which is an important dimension of household welfare, and examined the current

Table 3.4 Poverty estimates by infrastructure and linkage model

	SHG member	Non-member	
Poverty profile for <1 km from paved road			
N	297	15	
Headcount ratio (%)	78.8	66.7	
Aggregate poverty gap per observation (Rs.)	132	139	
Poverty gap ratio (%)	38	40	
Foster-Greer-Thorbecke (squared poverty gap)	0.23	0.27	
Poverty profile for >1 km from paved road			
N	394	36	
Headcount ratio (%)	67.8	58.3	
Aggregate poverty gap per observation (Rs.)	116	109	
Poverty gap ratio (%)	33	31	
Foster-Greer-Thorbecke (squared poverty gap)	0.21	0.23	
Poverty Profile for SHG members by linkage	*Linkage 1*	*Linkage 2*	*Linkage 3*
N	86	497	108
Headcount ratio (%)	81.4	70.6	74
Aggregate poverty gap per observation (Rs.)	133	118	135
Poverty gap ratio (%)	38	34	39
Foster-Greer-Thorbecke (squared poverty gap)	0.21	0.21	0.26

Source: Bali Swain 2012.

Note
The Indian poverty line is defined as the proportion of households with per capita food expenditure of less than Rs.346.9 per month.

poverty status of households in SHG and non-SHG groups using various poverty measures. We further explored whether or not these households are currently vulnerable to future poverty.

Poverty indices and a vulnerability measure are estimated. Propensity score matching is then employed to control for the potential selection bias that may arise due to unobservable attributes. The treated and comparison groups are matched on the basis of their propensity scores, to estimate the average treatment on treated effect using nearest neighbour matching algorithm and local linear regression. Their robustness is checked with the help of sensitivity analysis and Rosenbaum bounds. The effectiveness in reducing vulnerability through SHG participation is further investigated using delivery mechanisms like different linkage models, or delivery to regions with more developed infrastructure.

Exploring the programme's impact on vulnerability, it is found that the household's ability to mitigate risk and cope with shocks is enhanced through SHG participation by increasing household earnings through provision of microfinance and training, aiding the household in the face of shocks by providing consumption loans, and enhancing their resilience by strengthening social support and improving women's empowerment.

Even though SHG-member households are found to be poorer than the non-SHG member (control group) households, they are not more vulnerable. Vulnerability is significantly lower for the more mature households as compared to the non-SHG members. Favourable initial conditions and enabling socio-economic environment, like better infrastructure, assist SHGs to be more effective in reducing vulnerability. Contrary

Table 3.5 Average treatment on treated estimates of SHG participation impact on vulnerability and average food expenditure per capita per month by infrastructure

Matching algorithm	Distance from	Paved road < 1 km	Distance from	Paved road > 1 km
	(1)	(2)	(3)	(4)
	Vulnerability	Food exp	Vulnerability	Food exp
LLR (bw 1)	−0.26*	−24.64	−0.19***	99.67
(S.E.)	(0.13)	(62.57)	(0.07)	(54.28)
LLR (bw 4)	−0.26**	−24.64	−0.19**	99.67
(S.E.)	(0.11)	(74.40)	(0.09)	(61.62)

Source: Bali Swain 2012.

Notes
** Significant at the 5% level. * Significant at the 10% level. LLR = local linear regression, *p*-values in parentheses standard errors created by 200 bootstrap replications.

Table 3.6 Average treatment on treated estimates of SHG participation impact on vulnerability and average food expenditure per capita per month by linkage model

Matching algorithm	Model 1		Model 2		Model 3	
	(1)	*(2)*	*(3)*	*(4)*	*(5)*	*(6)*
	Vulnerability	*Food expenditure*	*Vulnerability*	*Food expenditure*	*Vulnerability*	*Food expenditure*
LLR (bw 1)	−0.14	8.26	−0.14**	31.89	−0.04	67.58
(S.E.)	(0.09)	(50.49)	(0.06)	(37.37)	(0.11)	(124.47)
LLR (bw 4)	−0.14*	8.26	−0.14**	31.89	−0.04	67.58
(S.E.)	(0.08)	(52.57)	(0.06)	(33.39)	(0.11)	(145.86)

Source: Bali Swain 2012.

Notes

** Significant at the 5% level. * Significant at the 10% level. NN=neighbour to neighbour, bootstrap standard errors in parentheses. LLR = local linear regression, *p*-values in parentheses standard errors created by 200 bootstrap replications.

to expectations the type of linkage where the SHG is both financed and formed by the banks seem to be the most effective in reducing vulnerability.

The flexibility of a joint liability microfinance programme like SBLP permits the loan to be used for any purpose, production or consumption. SBLP thereby provides the participating households with the possibility for consumption smoothing thus reducing the variability in food consumption levels and hence vulnerability. It strengthens mutual support networks that help reduce vulnerability of members and that of their households in ways that may not be adequately captured by the change in household earnings. These empirical results have important implications for the SHG programme, where policy makers may maximize the impact of SHG through provision of better infrastructural facilities and using the linkage model 2 where NGOs form the SHGs and banks provide them with finance.

4 Asset creation[1]

Introduction

The Rangarajan Committee on Financial Inclusion stated that the Self Help
Group Bank Linkage Programme is 'the most potent initiative since Independence for delivering financial services to the poor in a sustainable
manner'.[2] With the potential of SHGs proclaimed in such an emphatic
manner, one would expect that existing evidence indicates substantial SHG
impact on borrowers. This chapter explores whether SHG participation has
long-term impact on member households through asset creation and if it
impacts parameters such as income. This is important since assets underlie
the structural determinant of poverty and studying asset composition can
help reveal the persistence of the underlying poverty status (Carter 2007).
Assets also help households to reduce their vulnerability to shocks, by
making individuals less subject to fluctuations in the short and medium
term (Hulme and McKay 2005).

In a simple pre-post comparison of SHGs in 1999 Puhazhendi and Satyasai (2000) find that the SHG's participation increased the average value
of assets per household (including consumer durables and livestock) by
72.3 per cent. All the interviewed members had savings in the post-SHG
phase as compared to 23 per cent of them during the pre-SHG period. The
average household savings also increased during this phase. Puhazhendi
and Satyasai (2000) also find a significant increase in resources spent on
income generating purposes, which they suggest could be one of the major
reason for the 33 per cent increase in average SHG households' income
between the pre-post period.

Another impact study on Indian SHGs is the Puhazendhi and Badataya
study (2002) commissioned by NABARD (India's rural development
bank) with 115 members and three states. They reported that the SHG participation led to an increase of 45 per cent in the households' assets. The
net average incomes of the SHG member households also increased by 23

per cent after SHG participation. The study measured impact by computing the percentage difference of the means of members' outcome variables
pre and post SHG membership. Clearly, this type of analysis does not
account for any changes in observable characteristics nor broad economic
changes through a control group.

Due to inappropriate corrections for selection bias, Tankha (2002) states
'their findings cannot be considered to be conclusive or even convincing'.
Nevertheless, this Puhazendhi and Badataya (2002) study has had much
policy influence, quoted by many sources and most recently by the RBI
(2008) paper on financial inclusion. Their results find that SHG membership significantly increases the asset structure (30 per cent), savings,
annual net income, employment (34 per cent) and social empowerment. As
a middle of the road assessment, CGAP (2006) claims SHG performance
as 'mixed so far', but admits to no real evidence. Still, CGAP proceeds to
assert that experience to date indicates that SHGs can serve as a viable
model, if implementation is competent.

The main results from the Rural Financial Access Survey (RFAS) 2003
World Bank survey were compiled in Basu (2006). They find that SBLP
significantly improved the asset position (livestock and consumer durables) of the sample households. The average increase in assets was about
72 per cent, from Rs.6,843 to Rs.11,793 in real terms (in one to three
years). About 59 per cent of the households saw assets increase after the
groups were formed. According to Basu (2006), before the groups were
formed, one in three households had no assets, however, after the groups
formation, this changed to one in six. Average savings per member more
than tripled, from Rs.460 before the group formation to Rs.1,444 after
SHG membership. The study also finds that the average net income per
household increased from Rs.20,177 to Rs.26,889. About 43 per cent of
the incremental income generated was from non-farm activities.

The 2006 EDA Rural Systems study (jointly with CRS (Catholic Relief
Services), CARE and GTZ; hereafter EDA) on 214 SHGs from 108 villages did not attempt an impact study but conducted interviews and focus
group discussions. The EDA survey finds that only about one-fifth of the
SHG members are non-poor. In many SHGs, SHPIs provide training and
outreach to members in fields such as primary healthcare, basic literacy,
family planning, marketing, and occupational skill training.

To explore the long-term dynamics of asset-creation in SBLP participants, Guérin *et al.* (2009) studied 495 SHG member households in
Tamil Nadu for a period of five years in three waves (2004, 2006 and
2009). They find that while 71 per cent of the households had increased
their assets, 22 per cent of the households had lost some of their assets.
For 7 per cent of the households there was no change in the financial

position. Of the 35.4 per cent respondents in the poverty margin, 11.7 per cent improved their assets whereas an equal number (11.8 per cent) lost theirs. For 10.9 per cent of the households, however, there was no change. According to Guérin *et al.* (2009), the impact of SHG programme on poor households is not conclusive as the proportion of families that improved their situation were almost the same as those whose position deteriorated.

National Council of Applied Economic Research (NCAER 2008) finds that the net income data collected from households reveal that households increased their net incomes by over 38 per cent between the pre and post SHG participation period. The average annual growth of the household income was 6.1 per cent after the SHGs linked up to the banks. The study also noted a slight decline in the share of income from agriculture and wages and salaries and a move towards livestock, self-employment, non-farm activities, including petty businesses, art and craft and professional activities.

Estimating impact on assets

As discussed in Chapter 2 the impact on assets is adulterated by the presence of selection bias due to unmeasured attributes. The decision to participate in SBLP depends on the same attributes that determine the assets. The potentially unobservable traits of the SHG members, such as higher entrepreneurial skills, ability to recognize opportunity, and other critical aspects, will make households more likely to participate in the SHG programme. However, these same traits would lead to higher asset creation even if they were not members of Self Help Groups. Ideally, for perfect impact assessment, one would choose a control group from the same village (which would hold all external conditions constant) but then earlier signees of SHGs may have different reasons for joining than later signees. Bias may also arise because policymakers may place programmes in better or worse off areas leading to non-random programme placement.

To hold the differences constant by drawing the treatment and control group from the same area, i.e. the same district, the differences in villages among the districts are controlled by choosing village specific variables. To account for non-members from these districts that may be availing themselves of district specific policies, such as parallel government programmes, the district fixed effects are used. To control the remaining village level variability, the village level characteristics are employed.[3]

Thus Bali Swain and Varghese (2009) use the Coleman pipeline methodology explained in Chapter 2 with SIAS data. They estimate the following regression:

$$A_{ijs} = a + \alpha X_{ijs} + \beta V_{js} + \lambda Ds + \gamma M_{ijs} + \delta \text{SGHMON}_{ijs} + \eta_{ijs} \qquad (4.1)$$

where A_{ijs} is the asset position for household i in village j and district s, X_{ijs} are the household characteristics; V_{js} is a vector of village level characteristics, and Ds is a vector of district dummies that control for any district level difference. Here, M_{ijs} is the membership dummy variable, which controls for the selection bias. It takes the value 1 for both old and new SHGs and the value 0 for those villagers that have chosen not to access the programme. The parameter of interest is δ, the causal treatment effect where SGHMON_{ijs} is the number of months that SHG credit was available to old members, which is exogenous to the households.

As suggested by Doss *et al.* (2007) the assets are divided into six categories: land owned, livestock wealth, dwelling and ponds, productive assets, physical assets and financial assets (includes savings and lending). Household characteristics include age, gender, education dummies and a shock variable.[4] The dependency ratios are included, as households with larger dependency ratios have greater incentive for asset accumulation. In order to control for initial wealth, land owned three years ago is also included.[5] For village characteristics, in addition to male wage, the following distance variables are also included: paved road, market, primary healthcare centre and bus-stop.

The empirical evidence provided in this section is based on the Bali Swain and Varghese (2009) study of SIAS data. Comparing old SHG members versus non-members find that they are of about the same age, with lower dependency ratio, similar level of education and a lower amount of land on average. In terms of village level variables, old SHG members are closer to most amenities but non-members are relatively closer to banks.[6] In comparing old SHG members to non-members on other variables, they further find that old SHG members on average have a relatively higher income, own less land and dwelling which translates into a lower amount of assets. Table 4.1 provides the regression results of Equation (4.1) for various specifications of the asset variable (Bali Swain and Varghese 2009). In column (1), the results for the gross assets specification are presented, whereas column (2) uses the same gross assets specification though the member dummy is dropped. To account for complementary borrowings, the recent liabilities are subtracted from all sources to obtain a measure of net assets in column (3). Column (4) explores the impact without SHG savings.

The results consistently yield significance of the member variables and the SHGMON variable. The significance for the member dummy indicates that SBLP members are on average less wealthier than non-members, holding everything else constant. It would take close to six years of

Table 4.1 Estimates of impact on asset creation ($\times 10^3$)

	(1) Gross assets	(2) Gross assets	(3) Net assets	(4) Gross assets – SHG savings
Member	-45.43 (2.36)**	–	-46.86 (2.44)**	-45.45 (2.34)**
SHGMON	0.649 (1.99)**	0.434 (1.35)	0.625 (1.92)*	0.625 (1.92)*
Age (years)	0.125 (0.22)	0.195 (0.34)	0.135 (0.23)	0.128 (0.22)
Gender (Female=1)	9.667 (0.74)	11.91 (0.91)	9.760 (0.74)	9.154 (0.71)
Dep. Ratio	38.17 (2.01)**	34.83 (1.89)*	37.57 (2.01)**	38.80 (2.05)**
Primary education	24.35 (2.00)**	25.70 (2.05)**	25.65 (2.12)**	24.06 (1.97)**
Secondary education	28.87 (2.42)**	28.14 (2.37)**	29.83 (2.52)**	28.48 (2.39)**
College education	57.06 (2.12)**	56.34 (2.06)**	59.01 (2.18)**	56.48 (2.11)**
Land 3 years ago (acres)	43.13 (8.11)**	42.82 (8.09)**	43.12 (8.08)**	43.08 (8.10)**
Average shock	2.297 (0.19)	2.223 (0.18)	8.118 (0.83)	2.024 (0.16)
Distance paved road (km)	-8.088 (2.55)**	-8.435 (2.63)**	-8.556 (2.69)**	-8.043 (2.54)**
Distance bank (km)	0.741 (0.65)	0.687 (0.61)	0.829 (0.72)	0.745 (0.65)
Distance market (km)	-1.835 (1.64)*	-2.004 (1.76)*	-1.909 (1.71)*	-1.820 (1.63)*
Distance healthcare (km)	1.661 (0.68)	2.064 (0.85)	1.863 (0.76)	1.614 (0.66)
Distance bus stop (km)	5.173 (1.65)*	5.535 (1.74)*	5.486 (1.74)*	5.152 (1.64)*
Male wage (Rs.)	-0.481 (1.05)	-0.374 (0.82)	-0.471 (1.03)	-0.473 (1.04)

Source: Bali Swain and Varghese 2009.

Notes

** Significant at the 5% level. * Significant at the 10% level. All regressions include district dummies. Analysis based on 842 observations. Absolute t-ratios in parentheses computed with White heteroskedasticity-consistent standard errors clustered by village. See text for definitions of variables.

membership to catch up to the initial wealth of non-members (assuming constant returns to participation). Of the household characteristics, the positive significance of the dependency ratio implies that households with a greater number of dependents are more interested in asset creation.

Education carries the expected signs in that households with greater education are more adept at asset creation (since no education is the dropped dummy). Initial wealth (as in the amount of land holdings) also influences the current asset position of a household. Of the village characteristics, distance from paved town and distance from market and bus stop (though very marginally) are significant. The district dummies (not shown here) are also significant at the 5 per cent level except for Koraput (at 10 per cent) and the districts in Maharashtra (Gadchiroli and Chandrapur).

Table 4.1, column (2) drops the member dummy. Bali Swain and Varghese (2009) find that the length of membership (SHGMON) is statistically insignificant. Coupled with the results from the selection corrected regression in column (1), this result indicates that improperly accounting for selection would lead one to incorrectly conclude that SHGs have no impact on asset creation. These results contrast with other impact studies (and the theoretical discussion) where member unobservables overestimate impact.[7] Many presume that microfinance borrowers are more entrepreneurial, etc. and are more likely to join credit organizations. However, we find these unobservable characteristics make borrowers more likely to join SHGs in part due to lack of access to other credit sources with SHPIs targeting them for these very reasons. Not taking these observations into account would underestimate impact.

As pointed out by Bali Swain and Varghese (2009) themselves, these results may raise the following two doubts. First, that longer SHG membership creates greater SHG savings since over a longer time period, SHG members have a longer time horizon to save. In this respect, some may argue that SHGs participation actually forces asset creation through encouraging this thrift mechanism. Table 4.1, column (3) indicates that the results are robust to this interpretation in that if we subtract SHG savings from assets, these assets represent wealth above the SHG savings requirement. A second doubt may arise for those who view credit as debt. This would then suggest that members may actually asset create but may also debt create by borrowing from other sources. In other words, their net position may deteriorate. Table 4.1, column (4) accounts for this observation by subtracting recent borrowing from all other sources by all household members. We find that SHG membership still matters for asset creation.

The assets were further disaggregated into the subcategories. Land value is doubtful as the source, due to the low turnover of land sales during years of membership. Other assets that members may accumulate include productive and physical assets. In additional regressions performed by Bali Swain and Varghese SHG membership does not create any impact on land value, business wealth or physical assets.

The disaggregated assets results from Bali Swain and Varghese (2009) are presented in Table 4.2. The output of other variables (shown in Table 4.1) is suppressed and focus is on the variables of interest, namely the membership and SHGMON variable. Tobit estimations are employed to account for the large amount of censoring.[8] The first column indicates results for the dwelling and ponds category and, though the SHGMON variable has no impact on this creation, these results indicate that SHG members have a lower ability to accumulate this variable. The second column indicates the positive impact on livestock accumulation. This result predicts some of the results on current income. The third column indicates a positive impact on total savings driven by SHG savings. Finally, the fourth column confirms that SHG members are not involved in credit cycling, i.e. borrowing from other sources in order to repay SHG groups. As the negative sign on the member coefficient of other borrowings indicates, members do not access other sources relative to non-members.[9] Old SHGs do not access other sources presumably because they have SHG access now. New SHGs presumably join SHGs because they cannot access other financial services.

Further results from Table 4.3 indicate the impact on current variables. Again only the results for member and SHGMON have been presented. The significance on total income indicates that members have higher income than non-members, though the length of membership (negative coefficient) has no impact. Results in column (2) (conditional on cultivator households) indicate that any impact on total income will not come from agriculture.[10] These results indicate the SBLP has resulted in engaging the members in activities other than pure agriculture towards other alternative

Table 4.2 Tobit estimates of impact on select disaggregated assets ($\times 10^3$)

	Dwelling	Livestock	Savings	Other borrowings
Member	−21.43 (3.72)**	−2.082 (0.89)	−0.721 (0.41)	−22.83 (3.10)**
SHGMON	−0.006 (0.08)	0.0070 (2.11)**	0.0461 (1.92)*	0.013 (0.11)

Source: Bali Swain and Varghese 2009.

Notes
** Significant at the 5% level. * Significant at the 10% level. All regressions include the right-hand side variables of Table 4.1 and district dummies. Analysis based on 842 observations. Absolute *t*-ratios in parentheses. See text for definitions of variables.

Table 4.3 Estimates of impact on select income variables (×10³)

	Total income	Agricultural income	Other income
Member	4.277 (1.68)*	4.844 (1.59)	−0.488 (1.42)
SHGMON	−0.068 (1.56)	−0.139 (3.21)**	0.019 (3.83)**
N	842	733	842

Source: Bali Swain and Varghese 2009.

Notes
** Significant at the 5% level. * Significant at the 10% level. All regressions include the right-hand side variables of Table 4.1 and district dummies. Absolute *t*-ratios in parentheses. Other income is a Tobit regression. See text for definitions of variables.

methods of income generation. This is confirmed by the results in column (3). Bali Swain and Varghese (2009) find a high impact of membership on other sources of income. These other sources of income include the following: livestock, fisheries, rent, forest, financial gain and salary income. In other regressions (not reported here), they also found no impact of length of membership on business profits (self-employment revenue minus costs) and total expenditure. These results are a bit disappointing for those that were hopeful of the SHG groups creating profitable microenterprises. However, the second results confirm the previous results that SHG membership has a limited short-term impact.

Bali Swain and Varghese (2009) investigate the impact of household level variables and explore the impact of other factors affecting assets and income. They explore whether office bearers of the Self Help Groups have greater influence and capture much of the surplus from SHGs. They also examine whether certain linkage model types favour greater asset creation. These results, presented in Table 4.4, column (1), confirm the anecdotal evidence from the EDA study that officers actually serve SHGs without capturing any undue amounts for asset creation (since office bearer is insignificant). This result may occur because SHG officers are elected officials of the group and not appointed by village chiefs or contacts, and also approved by the SHPIs.

Column (2) indicates that the linkage model type does not matter (since all the coefficients are insignificant) for asset creation (where the reference dummy is the most popular linkage 2 which is bank financed/NGO formed). It is found that linkage 2 does not have any advantages over bank formed (linkage 1) or bank financed/NGO formed (linkage 3) in terms of asset creation. However, evaluating the model per se is limiting since some of the models provide development and business training while others do not. For instance, usually banks might be more focused on group formation

Table 4.4 Augmented estimates of impact on asset creation ($\times 10^3$)

	Office bearers	*Linkage type*	*Linkage*training*
Member	−45.85 (2.37)**	−45.96 (2.31)**	−42.30 (2.19)**
SHGMON	0.593 (1.80)*	0.663 (2.02)**	0.478 (1.46)
Office bearer	6.620 (0.67)	–	–
Linkage 1	–	−19.83 (0.78)	2.745 (0.10)
Linkage 3	–	10.07 (0.78)	−0.483 (0.05)
Linkage 1*training	–	–	−22.99 (1.74)*
Linkage 3*training	–	–	87.77 (1.90)**

Source: Bali Swain and Varghese 2009.

Notes
** Significant at the 5% level. * Significant at the 10% level. All regressions include the right-hand side variables of Table 4.1 and district dummies. Absolute *t*-ratios in parentheses. See text for definitions of variables.

and providing financial services only, as they might not have the capacity or mandate to engage in skill training, etc. NGOs, on the other hand, may provide development and skill training.

For column (3), the training variable (number of weeks of training) is interacted with the linkage type, with the most dominant linkage model 2 as the base. The results show that with the NGOs direct involvement in the funding process and provision of training, there is a positive impact on asset creation. However, when the NGOs are not involved in the process at all (as in linkage model 1), this negatively impacts asset creation with respect to linkage 2. Since the results with linkage type alone are not significant, these results indicate that training must be provided by the NGOs at the same time for a positive impact on assets. Apart from SBLP, several NGOs are engaged in other development activities, which might result in additional skill training and opportunities for SHG members linked by them. The provision of training under the SBLP and its impact is discussed in greater detail in Chapter 6.

Conclusion

In this chapter, we evaluated the effect of Self Help Group participation on a long-term impact parameter, namely asset creation. By comparing the impact on current borrowers vis-à-vis self-selected new members that will be bank linked in the future, the evidence shows that longer membership duration in SHGs positively impacts asset creation. These results are robust to various specifications of assets. However, there was no evidence for impacts on short-term variables such as total current income. The impact on asset accumulation arises from the savings requirement in the programme and livestock accumulation which then leads to income diversification.

Comparing these results with the earlier studies (Puhazendhi and Badataya 2002), Bali Swain and Varghese (2009) evaluate the magnitude of the impacts. These results are calculated at SHGMON means and old SHG variable means. As a 30 per cent return to assets of SHG membership in the earlier study, Bali Swain and Varghese find a 15 per cent return. As with the earlier study, the latter study based on SIAS also finds a positive impact on savings (about 50 per cent). Bali Swain and Varghese find a positive impact on livestock, though the return is only about 4 per cent. However, in contrast to some of the earlier studies, Bali Swain and Varghese did not find a positive impact on income but they did find a movement towards diversifying income streams (a fall in agricultural income of 27 per cent but a rise in other income of 65 per cent.

The results of this study deviate from other impact studies. In particular, we find impact of microcredit membership whereas most of the studies reviewed in Goldberg (2005) show no impact at all. The unobservables matter and not introducing them can move the bias in an unexpected direction: underestimation of impact. Due to time limitations, impact studies may focus on short-term variables such as consumption and income. Older programmes such as SHGs allow researchers to analyse longer-term impact variables such as asset creation.

This study also yields some programme specific lessons. Linkages between banks (even public sector ones) and NGOs may provide effective means for credit delivery. In the predominant linkage 2, banks provide the funding and NGOs provide the training. However, the discussion in this chapter reveals that in terms of impact on asset accumulation, linkage 3 (where the funding is channelled through NGOs) is the most effective. To a certain extent the recent explosion of MFIs in the SBLP and their exponential growth may be a positive development in this regard. The time for which the borrowers have to wait for loans allows them to build up savings in order for the banks to trust the groups. The training that NGOs provide also help the rural households move away from pure agriculture and diversify to other sources of income. The NCAER (2008) study indicated a slight decrease in the income share from agriculture with a move towards livestock, self-employed non-farm activities as well as petty business, arts and craft, etc. The Bali Swain and Varghese (2009) study supports this with empirical evidence on a movement towards diversifying income streams. SBLP thus creates asset accumulation and can contribute positively towards income generation through further diversification into non-farm activities. In fact the World Bank (2009) also suggests this for the rural populations of the transforming countries like India, where with the declining contribution of the agricultural sector to the GDP, there is a greater need for finding alternative employment for the rural populations in the non-farm sector.

In terms of the relating asset accumulation to poverty, livestock and savings accumulation are more structural and long term and not as subject to the vagaries of annual weather patterns that would affect traditional agriculture. The results do not indicate whether asset accumulation is a superior exit strategy to other options. In fact, the low magnitude of live-stock returns, suggest that other options may be considered. For instance, consider a scenario where assets do not increase but profits do and these are redistributed towards children's education and health. A recent theoretical contribution by Ahlin and Jiang (2008) finds that long-run development from microcredit relies on saver graduation (due to gradual accumulation of average returns in self-employment).[11] They conclude that for microcredit to enhance broad-based development, it must depend on simultaneous facilitation of microsaving. The proposed Microfinance Bill has suggested regulatory changes in India that would permit savings through not just certain financial institutions but also through most MFIs, thus promoting microsavings.

5 Empowering women[1]

Introduction

Empowering women is perhaps one of the most frequently cited social objectives of most microfinance programmes. The SBLP was introduced as a core strategy for empowerment of women, in the Government of India's Ninth Plan (1997–2002) (Planning Commission 2002).[2] The impact of microfinance on women's empowerment however is difficult to verify. Women's empowerment is a multifaceted concept and an ongoing process, and defining it is in itself a challenging task. Moreover, women's empowerment is not directly observable and therefore difficult to measure.

Within the South Asian context, women's empowerment is viewed as a process in which women challenge the existing norms and culture, to effectively improve their well-being (Bali Swain 2007, Bali Swain and Wallentin 2009). Using this interpretation, this chapter investigates the impact of microfinance on empowering women, using 2000 (by recall) and 2003 SIAS data.

Empirical evidence from earlier research substantiates that the economic and social impact of microfinance empowers women (Bali Swain and Wallentin 2009, Pitt and Khandker 1998, Pitt *et al.* 2006, Armendáriz and Morduch 2010, Anderson and Eswaran 2005, Goetz and Gupta 1996, Dijkstra 2002, Beteta 2006, Bardhan and Klasen 1999). Investigating this further for SBLP we also examine whether it is the microfinance related economic factors or the non-economic factors that are more effective in empowering women.

Microfinance and empowerment

Access to credit has received even greater attention in the context of poverty reduction and women's empowerment objectives. With the aim to meet the Millennium Development Goals[3] and the role of microfinance programmes' in supporting it, there has been an increasing expectation on their impact on women's empowerment.

A majority of microfinance programmes target women with the explicit goal of empowering them. However, their underlying premises are different. Some argue that women are amongst the poorest and the most vulnerable of the underprivileged. As such, women in poor households are more likely to be credit constrained, and hence less able to undertake income-earning activities. Others believe that investing in women's capabilities empowers them to make choices, which is valuable in itself, and also contributes to greater economic growth and development. Another motivation is promoted by evidence from literature that shows that an increase in women's resources result in the higher well-being of the family, especially children. Finally, an increasing number of microfinance institutions prefer women members as they believe that women are better and more reliable borrowers, thereby contributing to their financial viability.[4]

Additional services like training, awareness raising workshops and other activities over and above the minimalist (financial services only) microfinance approach is also an important determinant of the extent of credit impact on woman's empowerment. In her study in rural Kenya Holvoet (2005) finds that in a direct bank-borrower minimal credit system, women do not gain much in terms of decision making power within the household. However, when loans are channelled through women's groups and are combined with more investment in social intermediation, substantial shifts in decision making patterns are observed. This involves a remarkable shift in norm-following and male decision making towards more bargaining and sole female decision making within the household.[5]

Most microfinance programmes empower their clients through direct and indirect strategies. Direct empowerment through microfinance takes place when women become members of a group and/or when they are exposed to training or workshops intended to foment greater awareness and self-esteem. Belonging to a group leads to the creation of further social capital and a support structure (of other group members) that empowers women to improve their overall (not just economic) wellbeing. Furthermore, most microfinance programmes encourage frequent group meetings, interactions with loan officers or bank officials, and the keeping of financial records, all of which tend to encourage discussions on issues related to economic activities and other household and village matters, not to mention stimulating greater mobility, literacy and personal confidence. Coupled with training and workshops designed to promote greater 'awareness' among women of their political, social and economic circumstances, it is anticipated that women will acquire the motivation and capacity to improve their personal situations within their households, communities and societies.

Microfinance also leads to an increase in women's empowerment through indirect channels. Access to microfinance nominally encourages and enables members to create income generating possibilities for themselves. By increasing the relative value of female time and money income, microfinance can enhance woman's bargaining and decision making power within the household.

In a collective decision making model, Browning and Chiappori (1998) show that if behaviour in the household is Pareto efficient, the household's objective function takes the form of a weighted sum of individual utilities. The individual weights can represent the bargaining power of the female members in the household relative to the male household members, in determining the intra-household allocation of resources. In the literature it is assumed that by increasing the relative value of women's time and income, the weight and hence the bargaining power of the female members can be increased within the household. This 'weight' may also be altered by social pressure. The weight parameter may thus reflect women's power in decision making in the household and may be one index of women's empowerment.

Several empirical studies have documented that women's access to credit contributes significantly to an increase in women's income, their likelihood of increasing asset holdings in their own names, better nutrition, health and education among their children, lower fertility, higher mobility, and increased political and social participation (see Armendáriz and Morduch (2010) for a useful review).

Others argue that the impact of microfinance programmes are limited for women as they undertake heavier workloads and repayment pressures for only small gains in income. Researchers have also suggested that loans taken by female borrowers are sometimes used by men in the family to establish enterprises. In such cases the women end up being employed as unpaid family workers with little benefit and greater debt burdens. For instance, Goetz and Gupta's (1996) investigation of loan use from credit institutions in Bangladesh found that a significant proportion of women's loans were controlled by male relatives.

Some researchers further contend that microfinance can reinforce women's traditional roles instead of promoting gender equality. Women's practical needs are closely linked to unequal gender roles, responsibilities and social structures. As such, any improvement in their economic situation may simply enable them to perform their normative gendered duties more efficiently.

Mayoux (1997) argues that the impact of microfinance programmes on women is not always positive. For women that have set up enterprises, women benefit from only small increases in income at the cost of heavier workloads and repayment pressures. Sometimes their loans are used by men in the family to set up enterprises, or sometimes women end up being employed as unpaid family workers with little benefit. She further points out that in some cases women's increased autonomy has been temporary and has led to the withdrawal of male support. It has also been observed that small increases in women's income are also leading to a decrease in male contribution to certain types of household expenditure. Rahman (1999) using an anthropological approach finds that between 40 per cent and 70 per cent of the loans disbursed to the women are used by the spouse and that the tensions within the household increases (domestic violence).

Mayoux (1997) further discusses how the impact within a programme also varies from woman to woman. These differences arise due to the difference in productive activities or different backgrounds. Sometimes, programmes mainly benefit the women who are already better off, whereas the poor women are either neglected by the programmes or are least able to benefit because of their low resource base, lack of skills and market contacts.

For instance, Harper in (Dichter and Harper 2007) recounts:

> The group to which I was talking pointed to a young mother who was sitting disconsolately nearby with her child who was clearly unwell. A few months earlier her husband had been killed in an accident in a nearby town where he was pedalling a rickshaw. After some weeks his wife asked her group if she could have a loan to buy medicine for her sick child, but to her surprise they told her that she already had an outstanding loan. Unknown to her, the group had given a loan to her husband's family; what was worse, it was overdue and they demanded that she repay it. She left the group without paying, and had ever since been more or less ostracized by the whole village.

Mayoux (2001) also warns about the inherent dangers in using social capital to cut costs in the context of other policies for financial sustainability. The reliance on peer pressure rather than individual incentives and penalties may create disincentives and corruption within groups. Reliance on social capital of women clients along with increasing emphasis on ideals of strict economic accounting at the programme level require increased voluntary contribution by the members in terms of time and effort. It has been noted that those putting in voluntary contributions also expect to be repaid in the form of leadership of the group, etc.

Finally, empowerment is a process, thus it may take a long time before the impact of the microfinance programme is significantly reflected on the observable measures of women's empowerment.

Defining women empowerment in the South Asian context

Empowerment has become so inclusive a concept that it has arguably lost its meaning. Parpart *et al.* (2002) explain that empowerment is based on an understanding of social change that is transformational rather than transactional in nature. Thus reductionist, essentialist and economistic explanations are inadequate and a more integrated approach is required.

Krishna (2003) defines empowerment as:

> the process of increasing the capacity of individuals or groups to make choices and to transform those choices into desired actions and outcomes. Central to this process are actions which both build individual and collective assets, and improve the efficiency and fairness of the organizational and institutional context which govern the use of these assets.

Empowerment is also related to the concepts of social capital and community driven development. As Krishna (2003) points out, empowerment by nature is a process and/or outcome. Social capital on the other hand features social organization such as networks, norms and inter-personal trust that facilitate coordination and cooperation for mutual benefit; it is by nature a stock. Community development gives control of decisions and resources to community groups; thus it is by nature an activity.

Kabeer (1999) explains that women's empowerment refers to the process by which those who have been denied the ability to make strategic life choices acquire such ability. This ability to exercise choice incorporates three interrelated dimensions: resources which include access to and future claims to both material and social resources; agency which includes the process of decision making, negotiation, deception and manipulation; and achievements that are well-being outcomes.

Bali Swain (2007) argues that woman empowerment is the process in which women challenge the existing norms and culture of the society in which they live to improve their well-being effectively. As explained in Bali Swain (2007) and Bali Swain and Wallentin (2009), not all activities that lead to an increase in the well-being of a woman are necessarily empowering in themselves. For instance, an activity like improvement in the nutrition of children leads to greater efficiency in women's household chores, but it also falls within the existing social norm that assigns women's primary role as a caregiver and household manager within the South Asian context (Kabeer 1999). When a woman is better able to perform such activities, it can lead to an increase in her self-confidence and feeling of well-being and may therefore create conditions leading to her empowerment, but the improved nutrition of children is not necessarily empowering on its own. As Cheston and Kuhn (2002) also argue, increased self-confidence does not automatically lead to empowerment, but it may contribute decisively to women's ability and willingness to challenge the social injustices and discriminatory systems that they face. This implies that as women become financially better off their self-confidence and bargaining power within the household increases and this indirectly leads to their empowerment.

Similarly, community development scheme initiatives that are undertaken by the SHGs, such as providing a more accessible safe water source in the village, can reduce women's unpaid work burden while leading to the better health of all household members, particularly children. However, such activities are for the welfare of the household (including women) and the community at large but are not directly empowering in themselves (Krishna 2003). In fact, they can help maintain the existing gender roles within a given society. Thus, the truly empowering activities are those that reflect the changes that women have effectively made to improve the quality of their lives by resisting the gender-based traditions and norms that reinforce gender inequality. Thus, for instance, if a woman offers greater resistance to any form of abuse from her husband or family, it may be considered that she is exerting for her well-being and is thus on the way to being empowered.

Measuring women empowerment

Like cognitive skills and quality of life, women's empowerment is a concept that cannot be measured directly. Given the complexity of defining women's empowerment it is not surprising that only a few empirical studies have tried to examine the impact of microfinance on women's empowerment.

The interpretation of women's empowerment and its measurement also varies across different studies. Most researchers construct an index/indicator of women's empowerment. While this might take into account an important aspect of women empowerment, it still suffers from the arbitrary assignment of weights to variables used in constructing the indicator of women's empowerment which are ordinal in nature for they are based on qualitative responses that are categorical in nature. Therefore, assigning a numerical value to these categories and using that to construct an indicator is inappropriate.

Ackerly (1995) for instance, created an indicator called 'accounting knowledge' that measures the probability that the changes associated with empowerment matter. Goetz and Gupta (1996) make an important contribution through their qualitative and quantitative analysis to examine the complicated household dynamics and underlying notion of empowerment in the context of the household decision making process. However, their index of Managerial Control to classify the borrowers into five categories ranging from no control to full control of the use of the loans has similar limitations.

In another study, Hashemi *et al.* (1996) investigate the change in women's empowerment with the help of an ethnographic study and quantitative survey of the Grameen Bank and Bangladesh Rural Advancement Committee (BRAC) in Bangladesh. The authors create an empowerment indicator that builds on eight attributes, namely mobility, economic security, ability to make small purchases, large purchases, involvement in major household decisions, and relative freedom from domination by the family, political and legal awareness, and participation in public protests and political campaigns; this is constrained by similar problems.

Measuring women's empowerment by constructing indices is an inappropriate technique as it allows the use of arbitrary weights. Most researchers, for instance, will agree that the impact of a woman's decision to buy cooking oil for the family is different in nature from her participation in a decision to buy a piece of land. Both these decisions have different implications and magnitude of impact on her empowerment. As such giving equal weight to both these decisions does not make sense. Similarly, suggesting an arbitrary weight for these decisions may seem inappropriate, since it is not for the researcher(s) to decide which factors and to what extent they contribute to women's empowerment.

In a comprehensive study, Pitt *et al.* (2006) use Item Response Theory (IRT), where the element of analysis is the whole pattern of a set of binary indicators that proxy for woman's autonomy, decision making power, and participation in household and societal decision making.[6]

Several studies, including Pitt *et al.* (2006) and Frankenberg and Thomas (2001), make a case for using data on attitudes of and towards women within the household. The SIAS data used in the analyses for impact of SBLP on women empowerment is self-reported, subjective and ordinal in nature. Bali Swain and Wallentin (2009) argue that it is important to recognize that appropriate methodology is used to treat it. They explain that ordinal variables have categories as values, which cannot be treated like a continuous variable.[7] Moreover, given the different categorical responses, it is difficult to compare the degree of response choices, even if the respondents choose the same response. Another limitation of previous empirical studies has been the use of estimated latent scores as observed variables in order to establish the relationship between the credit programme and women's empowerment. Finally most studies in the past have analysed the household data by trying to establish the empowerment at the individual level. There is a need for studies to estimate a more general equation model which can estimate the change in women's empowerment for the whole group.

Conceptual framework

The analysis in this chapter is based on the SIAS household data. Both the 2003 and the 2000 by recall are used for this purpose. A total household sample of 961 only women respondents was used. The sample includes a group of SHG members who have participated in the programme (805) and a control group (156).

Empowering women through SHGS

Bali Swain and Wallentin (2009) estimate a 'general structural model' that is arguably a more appropriate scientific methodology to estimate the impact of microfinance on women's empowerment. The path diagram of the general women's empowerment model is presented in Figure 5.1. The latent women's empowerment variables for 2000 (WE00) and 2003 (WE03) are represented by the ellipses in the diagram. These latent variables are measured by their respective indicators (in rectangles). The arrows in Figure 5.1 represent the relation between the latent variable (women's empowerment) and their indicators as described by the measurement and the structural model. The measurement model measures the latent 'women empowerment' variable using indicators based on the definition of women's empowerment (Bali Swain 2007). Using Robust Maximum Likelihood technique the structural model analyses whether women empowerment takes place over time. Measuring women's empowerment is operationalized through a series of economic, behavioural, social and political indicators.

The analysis is based on longitudinal data on various indicators of women's empowerment for 2000 (by recall) and 2003. Women's empowerment encompasses different spheres of a woman's life. Literature on intra-household bargaining suggests that exogenous increases in female share of any income may be interpreted as providing the women with more power within the household. Hence participation in the labour market and greater economic independence leads to empowerment. This is proxied by the primary economic activity that the respondent is engaged in and the degree of the respondent's control over her own independent savings. It is assumed that an economically active woman with her own independent

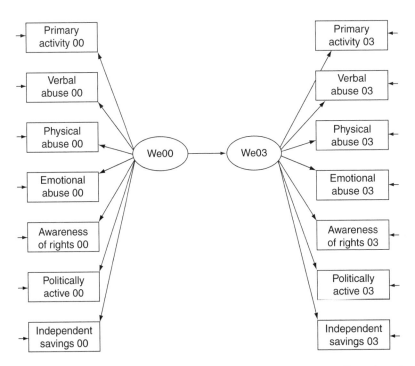

Figure 5.1 Path diagram for women empowerment model (source: Bali Swain and Wallentin 2009).

savings has more economic power and thus a higher bargaining power within the household, thereby making her more empowered (Ashraf *et al.* 2006) and likely to challenge the prevailing norms that restrict her ability to make choices.

Based on Bali Swain's (2007) definition, behavioural changes within the household that are meant to improve women's well-being are also crucial indicators of empowerment. This is especially important because a growing body of literature has begun to question whether microfinance really does lead to empowerment of women, especially if women continue to make choices that fall within the scope of the traditional roles that are rewarded by the society they live in. In the household survey respondents were asked questions on what they would do if they were: verbally abused; physically battered; and psychologically/emotionally abused within their family? In response to these questions the respondents made ordinal choices to reflect their degree of resistance or submission, which is a more direct reflection of their empowerment status within the household. For instance, the respondent could choose to reply with any one of the following options: resisted; submitted myself; lodged a complaint in the group or took their help; complained to relatives; or warned or did nothing.

A woman's participation in the political space is also an important indicator of empowerment. The SIAS household respondents were asked if they were aware that women had reservations in the local political institutions called Panchayats. They were also interrogated on their involvement in village politics, such as running as candidates or voting in local elections. Information on these two indicators were used as proxies for the 'political activism' aspect of women's empowerment. Other aspects of empowerment that were taken into account involved decision making roles regarding their work and household matters, as well as their mobility and participation in social networks. Although information on these two aspects of empowerment is available for 2003, the questions were not asked for 2000. Due to this data constraint it is expected that there will be a downward bias in the estimated impact of the Self Help Group programme over time.

Investigating the impact of microfinance participation on women's empowerment the data was analysed for two sub-samples, namely SHG members group and a control group comprised of non-SHG members. Bali Swain and Wallentin (2009) find that the estimated variance of women empowerment decreased dramatically from 7.57 to 1.66 for the SHG members between 2000 and 2003 (see Table 5.1). Their results suggest that the population is more homogeneous in 2003, as compared to 2000. This further implies that the variation in the level of women's empowerment diminished, especially within the SHG members group, as the disparity in the empowerment among the SHG members decreased.

The results from the Bali Swain and Wallentin (2009) general structural model confirms that the mean difference which captures the increase in women empowerment for the SHG members was highly significant for programme group at 0.26. The estimated variance for the control group

Table 5.1 Estimated mean and covariance matrix for women empowerment, SHG members, sample size 805

	WE00	*WE03*	*Mean (t-value)*
WE00	7.57		0.00
WE03	2.04	1.66	0.26*** (17.73)

Source: Bali Swain and Wallentin 2009.

Note
*** reflects that the mean value is significant at 1%.

also declined from 0.33 to 0.20, however, the mean difference was statistically non-significant for the control group. These results indicate that there was a significant increase in the level of women's empowerment over time for the SHG members but no such change was observed for the members of the control group (see Table 5.2).

The difference in the means between the two time periods, as shown in Table 5.1, may be interpreted as an increase of 26 per cent in the level of women's empowerment on average for the group of SHG members. However, this is not the case since the means of women's empowerment for the year 2000 and 2003 cannot be determined on an absolute scale.[8] One can only estimate the mean difference between the women's empowerment between these two time periods.

Bali Swain and Wallentin (2009) provide supporting evidence of a general increase in women's empowerment among SHG members over time. This, however, does not mean that each and every woman who joined the SHG programme has been empowered or that they have been empowered to the same degree or that they all progressed at the same pace. Some of the women members might have been more empowered than other members within the SHG programme prior to their participation in this programme. But on average one can argue that SHG members have been empowered over this time period. A similar empowerment process, however, cannot be observed for the control group. The differences in the pace of empowerment are likely to be a result of various factors, such as household and village characteristics; cultural and religious norms within the society; behavioural differences between the respondents and their family members; and the kind of training and awareness programmes that the women have been exposed to. All these factors together are responsible for the empowerment process.[9] The nature and types of activities and the kind of programme to which the women are exposed critically determines how empowering the impact of the SHG is on women. Thus a minimalist microfinance approach may not be sufficient by itself if the main objective of the SBLP is women empowerment.

Table 5.2 Estimated mean and covariance matrix for women empowerment, control group, sample size 156

	WE00	*WE03*	*Mean (t-value)*
WE00	0.33		0.00
WE03	0.23	0.20	0.076 (1.71)

Source: Bali Swain and Wallentin 2009.

The SHGs empower women through various channels. By providing the members with better access to loans, the SHGs enable them to generate income, thereby increasing their bargaining power within the household. Many SHGs also provide their members with training or workshops that tend to create greater awareness amongst women and also give them the opportunity to update and learn new skills. Several SHG members in the focus group discussion also emphasized the support of other group members and regular meetings.[10] Support from the other group members often extended beyond the economic activities to help members with their personal and family problems. In certain cases, the group members even went to the extent of directly intervening at the personal and the family level in support of their group members.

Regular group meetings also provided SHG members with an additional forum to discuss and interact, thereby diminishing their sense of isolation. Participation in the SHG programme also brought its members in close contact with government officials, bank officers and workers in NGOs.

Factors empowering women

Supported by the household bargaining literature,[11] researchers attribute women empowerment to the economic empowerment by microfinance (Browning and Chiappori 1998). Browning and Chiappori (1998) argue that increasing the relative value of female time and her monetary income increases her bargaining power to allocate resources within the household and empowers her. It also leads to greater investment in education, housing and nutrition for children (Duflo 2003).

Others emphasize the social impact of microfinance on greater autonomy (Anderson and Eswaran 2005, Goetz and Gupta 1996), awareness and political and social inclusion (Armendáriz and Morduch 2010; Dijkstra 2002; Beteta 2006; Bardhan and Klasen 1999). SHG formation and frequent group meetings give women an opportunity to break out of the daily routine and discuss their similar burdens, share their problems, giving them the opportunity to analyse that the root causes go beyond individual fault or responsibility (Townsend 1999). The group interaction creates an environment where personal problems are revealed as social patterns and negative emotions may be blamed on the environment rather than the self (Summer-Effler 2002). Furthermore, the interaction with women both within the SHGs and with other members of the SHGs increases the exposure and confidence to articulate and pursue her interests (Purushottaman 1998). Improved networking, better communication and greater mobility also empower women (Bali Swain and Wallentin 2009). Browning and Chiappori (1998) suggest that social pressure may also alter the woman's power within the household decision making. Changes in the attitude of woman through social pressure from SHPIs and other group members can also change attitudes within the household, and can lead to greater empowerment.[12]

SHPIs and SHG interaction also encourages the women to become active participants in the public arena, strengthening their ability to pursue their interests by making them more inclusive in the society and local politics (Bali Swain 2007; Tesoriero 2005). Women are thereby empowered by increased female representation in local governments (Bardhan and Klasen 1999; Dijkstra 2002) and greater participation in voting, demonstrating and getting involved in political organizations, as well as informal organizations to solve community problems (Beteta 2006).

It is however important to note that empowerment is multi-locational, exists in multiple domains and is multi-dimensional. Thus, women's control over a single dimension, for instance, economic decision making, does not necessarily imply ability to make reproductive or non-financial domestic decisions (Malhotra and Mather 1997). This is why alternative development initiatives such as political quotas, awareness generation and property rights are as essential for empowering women (Armendáriz and Morduch 2010; Kabeer 2005; Deshmukh-Ranadive 2003).

It is also critical to note that due to the cultural and social constraints imposed on the women in developing countries, women's autonomy or personal accumulation of resources may not necessarily result in empowering women on their own. Based on a survey of 15 different programmes in Africa, Mayoux (1999) finds that the degree of women's empowerment depends on inflexible social norms and traditions. Evidence from Bangladesh reveals that credit taken by women might be used by the male household head, with women having limited control over their own investments (Goetz and Gupta 1996).

Finally, women empowerment is not just an outcome, but a process (Johnson 2005; Kabeer 1999). Moreover, factors such as legal and regulatory framework and social norms and culture also have a significant impact on the empowerment process (Beteta 2006). Interactions between the different dimensions and domains of women empowerment process also play an important role.

To estimate the impact of microfinance related economic and non-economic factors on the empowerment of women Bali Swain and Wallentin (2011) use a structural equation model (SEM). They estimate a model which is described by the path diagram in Figure 5.2. The model consists of two parts: Measurement and Structural part. The measurement model towards the right in Figure 5.2 measures the latent women empowerment variable (in ellipse) by its respective observed indicators (in rectangles).

These indicators capture the definition of women empowerment within the South-Asian context. The various latent components (economic and non-economic factors) of women empowerment are measured by the observed indicators (in rectangles) on the left side of Figure 5.2. The relationship between the latent factors and their respective observed variables is indicated by the arrows. For instance, the latent economic factor is measured by the observed indicators like: respondent's participation in economic activity; owning an independent saving account; respondent's share of household income; investment in home improvement; confidence to meet financial crisis; and arranging capital and other inputs. The measurement errors are represented by the arrows that point to each of the indicators.

Bali Swain and Wallentin (2011) measures the latent women empowerment variable with the observed decision making variables that indicate increased participation in the traditionally male-dominated areas where South Asian women do not usually have a say.[13] They find that about 22 per cent of the respondents indicate participation in family planning decision had increased, while 31 per cent reported use of birth control. Buying and selling of property shows an increased participation by 18 per cent of SHG members. Women members also reported an increased involvement (by 30 per cent) in sending daughters to school.[14]

The latent factors of women empowerment (economic, autonomy, network, communication and political participation, social attitudes and education) were measured by the observed indicators as presented in Table 5.3 (Bali Swain and Wallentin 2011). The first column corresponds to the variable names in Figure 5.2 and lists the observed indicators used to measure each of the latent factors. Column 2 gives the exact question that was asked of the SHG respondent. The coding of their responses is given in column (3) while the proportion of the responses to each of these coded categories is presented in column (4).

The economic factor was measured by the proportion of resources that the SHG members' control and the economic activities that they are engaged in. Most of the respondents were economically active and were predominantly engaged in agriculture and related activities. Around 91 per cent of members reported that they had independent savings which they controlled. The respondents were also substantially confident about meeting a financial crisis in the family (87 per cent) and arranging credit and other inputs in time of need (60 per cent). About 20 per cent reported substantial home improvements and repairs. Their degree of autonomy was represented by their independence in taking crucial work related decisions (60 per cent), planning and implementation related to work (50 per cent) and their resistance to psychological and emotional abuse (about half of them offered resistance in varied degree).

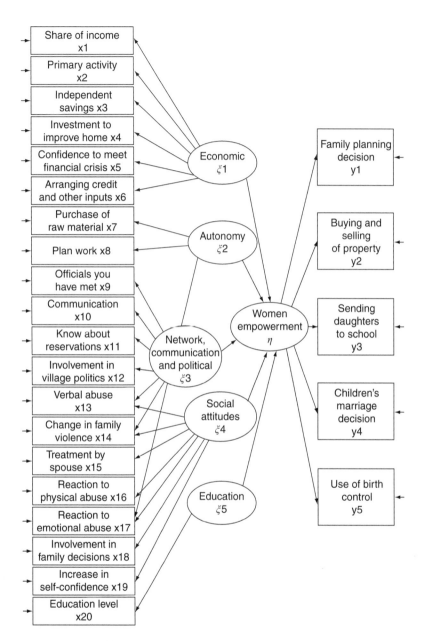

Figure 5.2 Path diagram for general women empowerment model (source: Bali Swain and Wallentin 2011).

Table 5.3 Description of observed indicators to measure latent variables[1]

(1) Observed indicators	(2) Questions asked to the SHG respondent	(3) Coding	(4) Proportion
1. Women empowerment			
Family planning decision	As compared to July 2000, has your involvement in the decision making on family planning increased?	1. Yes 0. No	1 = 0.22 0 = 0.78
Buying and selling of property	As compared to July 2000, has your involvement in the decision making of your children's marriage increased?	1. Yes 0. No	1 = 0.13 0 = 0.87
Sending daughter to school	As compared to July 2000, has your involvement in the decision making on buying and selling of property increased?	1. Yes 0. No	1 = 0.18 0 = 0.82
Children's marriage decision	As compared to July 2000, has your involvement in the decision making on sending your daughter to school increased?	1. Yes 0. No	1 = 0.30 0 = 0.71
Use of birth control	Have you used birth control?	1. Yes 0. No	1 = 0.31 0 = 0.69
2. Economic			
Share of household income	Respondent's income as a proportion of the household income	mean (std. dev.)	3.6 (26.2)
Primary activity	Primary activity of the respondent in 2003	1. Doesn't work 2. Farm activity 3. Self-employment in non-farm activity 4. Agricultural wage labourer 5. Non-farm employment 6. Others 7. No response	1 = 0.15 2 = 0.33 3 = 0.09 4 = 0.25 5 = 0.07 6 = 0.09 7 = 0.04

Independent savings	Does the respondent have independent savings which she controls?[2]	1. Yes 0. No	1 = 0.91 0 = 0.09
Investment to improve home	Has the respondent made any repairs, improvements or additions in their home that cost more than Rs.5,000?	1. Yes 2. No 3. Don't know	1 = 0.19 2 = 0.32 3 = 0.49
Confidence to meet financial crisis	Are you more confident of meeting financial crisis in the family after joining the group?	1. Yes 0. No	1 = 0.87 0 = 0.13
Arranging credit and other input	Are you able to arrange the credit and other inputs in time?	1. Yes 0. No	1 = 0.60 0 = 0.40
3. Autonomy			
Purchase of raw materials	Do you take crucial decisions in purchase of raw materials, pricing of the product of your activity?	1. Yes 0. No	1 = 0.60 0 = 0.40
Plan work	Do you plan your (work related) activities and get things done by others?	1. Yes 0. No	1 = 0.50 0 = 0.50
Reaction to emotional abuse	What would you do in the following situation in your family – psychological and emotional abuse?	1. Submit yourself 2. Do nothing 3. Resist 4. Give warning 5. Complain to relatives 6. Lodge complaint with SHG or take their help	1 = 0.08 2 = 0.43 3 = 0.23 4 = 0.10 5 = 0.05 6 = 0.12

continued

Table 5.3 continued

(1) Observed indicators	(2) Questions asked to the SHG respondent	(3) Coding	(4) Proportion
4. Network, communication, awareness and political participation			
Officials you have met	How many officials (from bank, government, etc.) have you met and spoken to?	Mean (standard deviation)	1.26 (1.5)
Communication	How does the respondent communicate in the meetings?[3]	1. Talks freely 2. Sometimes talks 3. Hesitates to talk and hence does not talk 4. Talks only if asked	$1 = 0.41$ $2 = 0.31$ $3 = 0.16$ $4 = 0.12$
Know about reservation	Do/did you know that women have reservations in panchayats and jobs?	1. Yes 0. No	$1 = 0.54$ $0 = 0.46$
Involvement in village politics	Do/did you get involved in village level politics?	1. Yes 0. No	$1 = 0.38$ $0 = 0.62$
Verbal abuse	What would you do in the following situation in your family – verbal abuse?	1. Submit yourself 2. Do nothing 3. Resist 4. Give warning 5. Complain to relatives 6. Lodge complaint with SHG or take their help	$1 = 0.18$ $2 = 0.21$ $3 = 0.35$ $4 = 0.06$ $5 = 0.02$ $6 = 0.18$
Change in family violence	Is there any change in family violence since July 2000?	1. Increased 3. No Change 2. Decreased 4. Never had any family violence	$1 = 0.10$ $2 = 0.05$ $3 = 0.21$ $4 = 0.65$

5. Social attitude

Item	Question	Responses
Treatment by spouse	As compared to July 2000 how is the treatment of your spouse towards you?	1. Less respectful $1 = 0.02$ 2. Usual $2 = 0.49$ 3. More respectful $3 = 0.50$
Reaction to physical abuse	What would you do in the following situation in your family – beating/physical violence?	1. Submit yourself $1 = 0.12$ 2. Do nothing $2 = 0.39$ 3. Resist $3 = 0.23$ 4. Give warning $4 = 0.08$ 5. Complain to relatives $5 = 0.03$ 6. Lodge complaint with SHG or take their help $6 = 0.15$
Reaction to emotional abuse	Refer above	
Involvement in family decisions	As compared to July 2000, has your involvement in all decisions of the family increased?	1. Yes $1 = 0.44$ 0. No $0 = 0.56$
Increase in self confidence	As compared to July 2000, has your self confidence	1. Increased $1 = 0.88$ 2. Decreased $2 = 0.03$ 3. Same as before $3 = 0.09$
Verbal abuse	Refer above	1. Submit yourself $1 = 0.18$ 2. Do nothing $2 = 0.21$ 3. Resist $3 = 0.35$ 4. Give warning $4 = 0.06$ 5. Complain to relatives $5 = 0.02$ 6. Lodge complaint with SHG or take their help $6 = 0.18$
Change in family violence	Refer above	1. Increased $1 = 0.10$ 2. No Change $2 = 0.05$ 3. Decreased $3 = 0.20$ 4. Never had any family violence $4 = 0.65$

continued

Table 5.3 continued

(1) Observed indicators	(2) Questions asked to the SHG respondent	(3) Coding	(4) Proportion
6. Education			
Education level	Education level in 2003	1. Cannot read or write	1 = 0.31
		2. No schooling but can sign my name	2 = 0.31
		3. No schooling but can read a letter	3 = 0.04
		4. No schooling but can read and write a letter	4 = 0.01
		5. Primary	5 = 0.12
		6. Secondary	6 = 0.18
		7. College	7 = 0.03

Notes
1 Source: Bali Swain and Wallentin 2011.
2 This variable has been constructed from the information collected on the savings of the respondent with and/or in: Self Help Group, banks, local chits, post-office, employers or others.
3 Surveyors made their own assessment about this question; however they were briefed in training of supervisors and surveyors with examples on how this assessment should be made.

Network, communication, awareness and political participation was measured by the number of officials that the respondent has spoken to, the communication skills of the respondent, their awareness and participation, in the local village politics and their reaction to abuse and mistreatment within the household. On average each member has met at least one official and most of them (72 per cent) were fairly confident in communicating and raising their concerns within the group meetings.

The 73rd constitutional amendment through the Panchayati Raj Act (passed in 1992) reserved one-third of local governance seats in India for women. Sinha *et al.* (2009) in their sample found that one in four SHGs had a member standing for election, one in five had a successful candidate. More than half of the elected representatives were active in carrying their responsibilities within the Panchayat. But the most active ones were those with political connections, or with a background of employment in government programmes, which gives them greater exposure and confidence. Bali Swain and Wallentin find that more than half the group members were aware of the reservations, in local political institutions and jobs, for women and 38 per cent had been involved in village level politics. Greater awareness in the respondents towards women rights was also reflected in their resistance to verbal abuse and domestic violence.

Social attitudes and changes therein were measured by the behaviour of the respondent's spouse towards her, her reaction to physical, psychological and emotional abuse that she may have been subjected to, and increasing resistance in reaction to such attitudes. Other measurement variables include the increase in the level of self-confidence (88 per cent) due to non-economic factors and greater involvement in all family decisions (44 per cent). Finally, the level of educational attainment in 2003 was measured by the contribution of education towards empowerment of women members.

Bali Swain and Wallentin's (2011) results confirm that the economic factor has the most significant impact on empowering SHG women (see Table 5.4). Loans provided within the SHGs enable members to create additional economic opportunities and generate income. It thereby increases their bargaining and decision making power within the household and leads to women empowerment. Greater autonomy in terms of independent planning, management and decision making at work and greater propensity for intolerance of negativity at home also significantly contributes to empowering women. Provision of managerial training and awareness creation activities by SHPIs lead to greater exposure and changes in social attitudes.

Social attitudes of the respondent, her spouse and other members of the household also play a critical role. Moreover, the process of group formation, frequent group meetings, support of group members and the involvement of SHG members in village development activities create confidence and changes in the attitude of the respondents and their household members.

Of these three significant factors, Bali Swain and Wallentin (2011) found empowerment by economic factor to be the most effective. In fact, the economic factor was twice as effective in empowering women as member's autonomy. The social attitudes were also crucial but were only about two-thirds as effective as the economic factors in terms of their contribution to women empowerment.

Education was statistically non-significant in their estimated model. As Stromquist (2002) explains, access to formal schooling does not necessarily lead to empowerment and women's empowerment is possible more through non-formal education programmes. The alternative spaces provided by women-led non-governmental organizations promote systematic learning opportunities through workshops on topics such as gender subordination, reproductive health, and domestic violence, and provide the opportunity for women to discuss problems with others. Networking, communication and political participation were non-significant though they may be critical in empowering in the long run. The statistical non-significance of some of these factors should not be interpreted as unimportant (Bali Swain and Wallentin 2011). Rather, it is expected that education, networking and political participation will indeed have a positive impact in the long run, which may not be observable in a span of a few years.

Table 5.4 Estimated parameters of women empowerment structural model for SHG members

Latent factors of women empowerment	Coefficients (absolute t-value)
Economic	0.54 (4.35)***
Autonomy	0.27 (2.42)***
Network, communication and political participation	0.067 (0.77)
Social attitudes	0.37 (4.09)***
Education	–0.071 (0.91)
Model fit	
Satorra-Bentler scaled Chi-Square	$\chi^2 = 806.44$ df$=257$
RMSEA	0.05
NFI	0.91

Source: Bali Swain and Wallentin 2011.

Notes
*** Significant at the 1% level. *t*-statistics in parentheses. Analysis based on 810 women SHG members.

Concluding discussion

The empowerment process is a challenging task for any individual, let alone those members of the society that are not only socially repressed but also economically weak. The results from Bali Swain and Wallentin (2009) derived from the application of the general structural model clearly indicate that on average there is a significant increase in women's empowerment of the SHG members' group. No comparable change is observable for the members of the control group.

Yet while the analysis clearly shows the evidence for a general increase in women's empowerment for SHG members over time, this does not imply that each and every woman who joined the SHG Programme was empowered to the same degree or that they all progressed at the same pace towards being empowered. It provides us only a general answer as to whether or not the SHG programme empowers women. It is difficult to ascertain which factors tend to be more important in empowering women.

Variability in the pace and degree of women's empowerment is due to a number of factors, such as household and village characteristics, cultural and religious norms, behavioural differences among the respondents and their family members, and the kinds of training and awareness initiatives to which women have been exposed.

Investigating further, Bali Swain and Wallentin (2011) evaluates whether economic or non-economic factors are more effective in empowering women participating in a SHG–bank linked programme. They find that economic factors have the greatest direct impact on empowering women. This confirms that programmes like SHGs which focus on income generation by women in low-income households have the double advantage of leading to an improved economic situation of the respondent and being the most effective factor in empowering women. Greater autonomy and changes in social attitudes also lead to empowerment of women, although the magnitude of their impact is relatively smaller than the economic factor.

Their empirical investigation reveals that with respect to the control of resources, changes in behaviour and decision making, women are in the process of empowering themselves. Focus on income generation should continue as the primary objective of the SHG programme. The results discussed in this chapter clearly indicate that participation in an economic activity, opportunity to access credit and arrange crucial inputs play a significant role in empowering women. Greater confidence to meet the financial crisis and having independent savings is also empowering. Thus, the provision of 'minimalist' microfinance through its economic impact remains the most important cause for promoting women empowerment of SHG member.

Social attitudes and push towards greater autonomy are also critical in empowering SHG members. Several researchers have stressed that provision of credit is not enough in itself, for greater empowerment women also need to control and take decisions related to their credit, resources and work (Anderson and Eswaran 2005; Goetz and Gupta 1996; Malhotra and Mather 1997). The SHPIs through the SHGs can make substantial contributions towards this by strictly monitoring that the loans are being used by the woman and not by others (or a male member) in her household. Microfinance 'Plus', with SHPIs providing additional services to the SHG member, should also be encouraged. SHPIs may undertake activities like informing SHG members about women's rights (legal, political and social), creating general awareness about improving attitudes towards women and introducing women to the existing government programmes and opportunities which they can access. Provision of education, increased political participation and better communication surely also have an important role to play in the long-run empowerment process. One limitation of these women empowerment studies is that they have evaluated the benefits through impact, but not estimated the cost. Perhaps other women empowerment programmes may successfully deliver the same level of impact at lower cost.

For long-term impact the success and sustainability of the SHG–Bank Linkage Programme is also very important. This crucially depends on creating and maintaining good quality SHGs. Both with regard to the impact on women's empowerment and the sustainability of the programme it is important to identify who are promoting the groups. As Basu and Srivastava (2005) point out, if NGOs with their social-development perspectives are entrusted with this task, they need to be paid for this role. If the banks (who are concerned with their business of financial services) are put in charge of this task, they might be more interested in ensuring the safety of their loans rather than taking time-consuming interest in managing the SHGs. Fisher and Sriram (2002) also caution that without proper monitoring and support the long-term sustainability of the SHGs is at risk. It is trivial to point out that without sustainable microfinance, provision of quality services and quality group, long-term impact will be difficult to attain.

If women's empowerment is to be pursued as a serious objective by the SHG programme in particular and the larger microfinance community in general, greater emphasis needs to be placed on training, education of women and creating awareness, with increased investment in social intermediation. Without these, channelling microfinance through women's groups alone might result in several other positive outcomes but will not translate into women's empowerment.

6 Building human capital through training[1]

Introduction

Whether it is women empowerment or long-term economic impact on participating households in the form of asset creation, so far the empirical evidence from SIAS points towards additional services, over and above the provision of microfinance. There has been an ongoing debate on 'minimalist' or 'microfinance plus' provision of financial services to the underprivileged.

MFIs that promote 'minimalist' microfinance focus on lending with the belief that membership by itself 'trains' participants in a number of ways. By working, saving and repaying, members adopt a disciplinary ethic. Members 'learn by doing' without any need of training by working on projects. Finally, regular meetings are expected to provide a setting for members to discuss and learn from others about their work related problems.

It is important to know if MFIs should teach skills (Karlan and Valdivia 2009) where some researchers and practitioners believe that households already have the human capital and only need financial capital. Others suggest that households cannot effectively use the financial capital that they receive without proper training and human capital skills. They further suggest that since MFIs have already organized borrowers to obtain loans, the cost of providing additional services is small. Thus MFIs are faced with a decision on whether they should branch out to training or just lend.

'Microfinance plus' combines the provision of credit with other important inputs like literacy training, farming inputs or business development services (Morduch 2000). Alternatively, the 'minimalists' argue that MFIs should focus on becoming sustainable and, to reach financial and/or operational sustainability and greater outreach, they should only provide financial services.

This chapter explores whether training of SHGs and building their human capital affects their outcomes over and above membership (which measures loan access). Two different outcome measures are employed to measure impact, a long-term (assets) and a short-term (income).

Puhazhendi and Badatya (2002), which was one of the first impact studies conducted by NABARD, reported that around 80 per cent of the surveyed members received some form of training. About 97 per cent of the SHGs that were formed by NGOs received training programmes, while only 50 per cent of SHGs formed by banks received such inputs. Of the surveyed members about 73 per cent of the respondents expressed satisfaction with the usefulness of training programmes.

In the impact and sustainability study of the SBLP, the National Council of Applied Economic Research (NCAER 2008) claims that SHGs have significantly improved the access to financial services of the rural poor. They also find that SHPIs provide training and outreach to members in fields such as primary healthcare, basic literacy, family planning, marketing and occupational skills, and that training improves members' skills such as communication, marketing and human development. However, they did not indicate whether the training translated into better outcomes. Their report on 4,600 households from six states in India measures impact as the compound annual growth rate of the outcome measure from pre to post SHG participation. Five of the six states of the NCAER study overlap with the SIAS data.

According to NCAER (2008) nearly half their surveyed SHGs received some form of human skill development. SHGs gave the highest priority and developed several of the following skills within their members that led to a positive impact on their livelihood and income generation possibilities. About 42 per cent of the survey households received the opportunity to develop their motivation skills, 40 per cent received leadership training while 30 per cent of the households got the opportunity to develop their communication skills. Management skills were relatively less developed. Also, members were involved in different activities as individuals rather than as a group. Common reasons that constrained group activities were listed as lack of markets for their products, weakness in competing with existing competition in the market and lack of required skills to work in activities other than agriculture or animal husbandry.

NCAER (2008) found that income increased by 6 per cent, assets increased 10 per cent and participants were more empowered.[2] These results were also confirmed by EDA Rural Systems (2006) that found a similar positive impact.

Clearly, the NCAER analysis does not account for any changes in characteristics or broad economic changes through a control group. Their study does not measure the effect of training on the SHGs but just mentions that it is inadequate. However, due to the limited number of large-scale impact research on SHGs, these types of studies have had much policy influence and quoted in Reserve Bank of India and National Bank for Agriculture and Rural Development publications. There exists a large body of literature on measuring the impact of training in general, which has been succinctly summarized in LaLonde (1995). Evaluation of training impact has been subject to a healthy debate on the effectiveness of matching estimators (see, for example, Smith and Todd 2005). However, most of this literature has been based on the data from developed countries and, in particular, from one training programme in the US. When accounting properly for selection bias, the studies find a positive impact of training.

Self Help Groups and training

Training and capacity formation in the SBLP can be broadly classified into two categories.[3] General training to all SHG members covers group formation and an introduction to linkage methods, which includes basic literacy, book-keeping, group formation and dynamics.[4] The general training usually takes one day and each participant is awarded Rs.250 (equivalent to a week of agricultural wages, a generous compensation). All participants receive this relatively homogeneous training to create the capacity within the group to sustain and manage the financial activities of the group. While this type of training is vital for SHG creation and its quality and sustainability, it is not the aspect of training that we intend to measure in this chapter.

SBLP also provides a range of heterogeneous training modules through SHPIs, especially NGOs. These include skill formation training, which aims at improving income-generating activities such as farming, craft or business. Sinha *et al.* (2009) explain that the NGOs and the government provide different types of development support, these include community mobilization and watershed and land development, campaigns on social issues, school construction, building village roads or small bridges, cleaning villages, installation of hand pumps, sanitation, enterprises, training and skills development, and market support (for instance, dairy), women's issues, anti-liquor campaigns and discussions in group meetings, and women and Panchayat Raj, inputs including training and information of group leaders on Panchayat Raj and elections, and motivation to vote and contest leadership positions.

The nature of this training is highly variable. Different SHPIs, whether NGOs, MFIs or government agencies, have different development objectives and programmes. Thus, they have an interest in focusing on different kinds of training programmes. This chapter focuses on examining the impact of such additional training that aims at generating a socio-economic impact. For the training programmes to be organized, first SHG members have to demand the required skill training. However, their demand is not met in many cases because the viability of the training sessions require a critical number of potential trainees to make the 'demanded' training programme cost effective. Moreover, SHPIs need to find local trainers for that specific skill. Since some of the demand is internally driven, members participate out of interest and need. Actually, many members other than those that initially request the training participate in the sessions. Furthermore, NABARD's stipend provides an added incentive to participate. The NCAER (2008) study finds that about 34 per cent of their surveyed households reported having developed market skills among their SHG members (a higher percentage of these were from linkage model type 2 and 3), whereas an even higher share of 40 per cent suggest a need for developing management skills. In fact 60 per cent of the members reported a need to improve their technical skills. They also found that about 80 per cent of the SHGs faced problems in members' skill development because of lack of time, lack of interest, low literacy level of the members and inadequate training facilities. Members reported required improvement in financial (59 per cent), management (40 per cent) and market development skills (33 per cent).

According to NCAER (2008), 50 per cent of the households received training for improving income generating activities such as farming, craft or business during the previous year (2006). About 35 per cent of the households received training only once, whereas 15 per cent of them received training multiple times.

Skill formation programmes include the REDP (Rural Entrepreneurial Development Programme), that are designed for unemployed but educated rural youth.[5] Other programmes such as Reach provides tools with training to improve their business planning and take advantages of new opportunities. Other than the REDP, some SHPIs also provide additional education, health and awareness creation training. In contrast to the base training, these additional modules of training are more haphazard and not homogeneous or focused. Thus, the training covered in this chapter is 'as delivered' and not optimal in any sense. This notion of training contrasts with the Karlan–Valdivia study where meetings started with training and with penalties such as fees for tardiness and threat of expulsion.[6]

There are different views on the relative advantages of SHGs over private MFIs in training delivery. Supporters of NGO linked SHGs (linkage model 2) assert that the NGOs perform effective development activities within their own district and are hence the best equipped to provide training services. Moreover, they do not need an extra incentive mechanism to monitor and train SHGs. If NGOs choose to deny training services to a particular group, then the NGOs have identified that group as low quality. It is also flexible in allowing the members to initiate training which differs from many standard Grameen style models.

During SIAS field interviews several bankers emphasized the importance of training. In fact the lead district manager of a renowned bank[7] suggested that skill training should be provided to the SHGs every three months so that they may improve their economic standard further by leading to suitable income generating activities.

In contrast to SHGs, several MFIs are donor driven and face pressure to obtain high repayment rates which may stifle their training efforts. In particular, training may have payoffs later but add to current costs and thus may damage current outcome measures. Since the government supports the SHG programme with a development mission in mind, it may not face the same pressure. The SHG model reflects a more mature institutional approach, while the private MFIs reflect a relatively market oriented outlook.

Measuring the SHG training impact

A popular methodology is the randomization method. Karlan and Valdivia (2009) use a randomized experiment in Peru, to find that business training improved business practices and revenues. Their results show that this increased knowledge led to greater repayments and client retention. Since they do not separately measure the effects of membership, their results hold conditional on membership. As discussed in Chapter 2, even though the scientifically robust randomization studies provide reliable results, they are weak on external validity since they study only one programme in one specific place. Thus, for SHGs in particular and for microfinance programmes in general, for developing countries, not many studies have analysed the contribution of training to outcome measures. Millions of rupees are spent on training by SHPIs every year and 60 per cent of the SHGs rely on outside support for training (NCAER 2008). It is therefore important to investigate if training has an impact that justifies this expenditure.

Bali Swain and Varghese (2010a) provide an alternative way by estimating training impact on SHG members when non-experimental data is available. Faced with a double selection problem, they first correct for the selection into the programme and later discuss the treatment of training endogeneity. The selection bias is rectified using a pipeline method while propensity score matching is used to correct for training.

The modified pipeline method that Bali Swain and Varghese (2010a) adopt is 'phased in randomization', a randomization method suggested by

Banerjee and Duflo (2009). In this method randomization is delayed over time. Simulating this Bali Swain and Varghese take the pre-selected borrowers that are denied access to loans for the first six months. In this way, the Coleman's pipeline method in effect adopts the core concept of a randomized experiment.

Bali Swain and Varghese (2010a) also check whether NGOs favour certain types of villages earlier than others for linkages. They argue that NGOs operate within villages without expecting to participate in SBLP and are motivated by their own development work. Checking and comparing different linkage models, they do not detect a difference in linkage choice of villages with old and new SHG members.[8] They conclude that NGOs do not favour certain villages first over others.

Training placement, as anticipated, is more complicated than the actual programme placement. Bali Swain and Varghese (2010a) examine if the more remote villages are less likely to have training programmes. Investigating this through logit regressions, they find that the distance from the paved roads affects training programme location, as well as level of male wages. Moreover, further the distance from the bus stop, the greater is the likelihood of a training programme.[9]

The training delivery is a multi-step process where the member has to first have a demand for training and then request it. Sometimes households that do not initially demand training may end up participating in the training session in their village. Finding a suitable trainer is another task resting on the hope that a critical mass of trainees demand that specific training.

Bali Swain and Varghese (2010a) then employ both matching and regression adjusted matching estimators as in Barnow *et al.* (1980) to adjust for both training and participation bias.

Trainings impact on SHG

Bali Swain and Varghese compare the means and variances of the training weeks for mature and new SHGs. They find that the amount of training weeks and variability in training is larger for mature. About half of the mature SHGs received training while 39 per cent of the new SHGs reported the same.[10] Bali Swain and Varghese (2010a) indicate that membership (evaluated at SHGMON means for mature members) provides a return of 15 per cent on assets. Their regression adjusted estimates suggest that training can double these returns. Their results clearly present conclusive evidence on the 'minimalist' and 'microfinance plus' debate. They argue that MFIs should not be focused on lending alone. On the contrary the regression adjusted estimates of income suggest that membership and training has no impact on income.

The lack of training impact on income generation contrasts sharply with the impact on asset accumulation. However, as mentioned earlier in Chapter 4, Bali Swain and Varghese (2009) also found a positive impact of SHG participation on asset creation but not on income. Within the SHG programme, the loans are not necessarily bound to be used for productive purposes and hence they may not provide a positive impact on income in the short run. Bali Swain and Varghese (2009) shows that SHG participation leads to a movement away from agriculture to livestock raising, thus indicating a potential transitional loss in current agricultural income but a possible gain in assets.

The thrift activities within the SBLP and training components helps the asset accumulation immediately but may not translate into a corresponding impact on income. The results from Bali Swain and Varghese (2010a) correspond to a recent large-scale randomized study from Indian slums where microfinance participation has had no impact on current variables such as consumption but borrowers have moved towards consuming more durable goods and starting new businesses (Banerjee *et al.* 2009). Generating income from new microenterprises requires time, and uncertainty in business and reliance on external markets add additional challenges which make success and a positive impact on income difficult to achieve.

SHGS, training and delivery mechanisms

Bali Swain and Varghese (2011b) further examine whether the impact of training on assets and income depends on the delivery mechanism, namely, linkage model type, infrastructure and training organizer. They investigate the impact of the quantity of training, in terms of the amount of weeks of training, on the borrowers on assets and income. Furthermore, they also examine if training is more effective in villages with better infrastructure and explore which linkage type and training organizer delivers the greatest impact for training.

SHPIs consist of NGOs, individuals, bank officers or government officers. These SHPIs link the Self Help Groups to banks through three linkage models. Model 1 encourages banks to form and finance Self Help Groups. Model 2 encourages NGOs to form groups but the groups are financed by the banks. In model 3, NGOs form groups and act as financial intermediaries for the groups. There are certain drawbacks of the linkage models. In model 1 banks may form groups for the sole reason of receiving bank loans and may disintegrate more quickly. Orientation of the bank officials to microfinance style lending is also a time and resource intensive process (Satish 2001).

Model 2, which is the most popular, reached the most of poor borrowers, since the groups were formed by NGOs. Not only does it requires coordination between banks and NGOs, it also exploits each SHPI's comparative advantage, with the bank's lending and NGOs focusing on group formation and training. In Model 3, NGOs act as MFIs, thereby implementing the twin tasks of forming the groups and linking them to loans. One would anticipate the greatest impact for model 2, where each institution follows its comparative advantage. The least impact is expected to arise for model 1, since the bank officials form groups with limited experience while in model 3, the NGOs that undertake additional duties and risk in lending directly to the SHGs.

Better infrastructure can support training and magnify its positive impact. For instance, lack of paved roads negatively impact communication and connectivity and may constrain the organization of a training camp within that village, or the possibility of finding a trainer who would be able to commute to the village easily. Trainers do not reside in the particular village but would travel to the village through transportation which is aided by access to paved roads. Bali Swain and Varghese (2011b) examined different variables to see which would affect the impact of training. They find that of all the infrastructure variables, only distance from paved road matters.[11] Recent research on the impact of rural roads finds similar evidence (Estache 2010). Thus, training effectiveness requires improvements in infrastructure to produce better impact of training.

They also examine whether the organizer of the training had a positive impact. Does the training impact vary by the provider, whether government official or worker or an NGO?[12] If training is organized and conducted by NGOs, members might implement the training programmes in a better way with more dedication.

The Bali Swain and Varghese (2011b) investigates the above questions and their empirical results are presented in this subsection. Table 6.1 summarizes the training statistics by model type. Interestingly, under linkage model 1 where banks form SHGs, the largest proportion of members

Table 6.1 Training statistics (by linkage model)

Training statistic	Model 1	Model 2	Model 3
Received training (%)	55	43	48
Length of training (weeks)	2.5 (1.4)*	3 (1.9)*	2.3 (1.5)*
Government training (%)	6.5	11.4	2.4
Training by NGOs (%)	89	70	76
Training organized by others (%)	0	1	0

Source: Bali Swain and Varghese 2011b.

Notes
* Mean (standard deviation).

receive training, but under the more popular linkage model 2 where NGOs form SHGs, the training period is longer per member. NGOs dominate training organization, even in linkage model 1. The regression estimates indicate that training positively impacts income but not assets. However, membership positively impacts assets and negatively income. The length of training has no direct impact on either income generation or asset creation. The results indicate that training may be more effective with a focused delivery, that is, higher quality and diversity.

Examining results by linkage type, with the model 2 as the reference category, Bali Swain and Varghese (2011b) find that model 3 has the most negative impact on income. As expected, model 1 combined with training also affects income negatively. They further find that the training organizer matters and their evidence shows that training held by the government can negatively affect asset accumulation.

When the results are further refined by correcting for selection bias due to the choice of participation in SHG and training, the regression adjusted matching estimates indicate that a breakdown by linkage type has no effect on assets (see Table 6.2). However, when it is the banks that form the groups it harms the SHGs' income generation. On the other hand, linkage models 2 and 3 (where the NGOs are actively involved) positively impact income.

The regression adjusted results further confirm that the training organizer and leaders matter. As suggested by Table 6.3, when NGOs organize

Table 6.2 Regression adjusted matching estimates[a] of training impact on assets and income by linkage model ($\times 10^{-2}$)

Matching algorithm	Model 1		Model 2		Model 3	
	(1) Gross assets	*(2) Income*	*(3) Gross assets*	*(4) Income*	*(5) Gross assets*	*(6) Income*
LLR (bw 1)	247.8	−122.8**	116.8	27.2	227.1	45.1*
(S.E.)	(501.6)	(50.8)	(119.5)	(18.5)	(171.2)	(26.8)
LLR (bw 4)	247.8	−122.8**	116.8	27.2*	227.1	45.1*
(S.E.)	(499.1)	(57.2)	(110.1)	(15.5)	(158.9)	(26.1)

Source: Bali Swain and Varghese 2011b.

Notes
** Significant at the 5% level. * Significant at the 10% level. LLR = local linear regression, *p*-values in parentheses standard errors created by bootstrap replications of 200.
a Covariates of regression are: number of months since a member has joined SHG; weeks of training; age; gender (female = 1); dependency ratios; primary education; land 3 years ago; distance from paved road; distance from bank (kms); distance from market; distance from healthcare; distance from bus-stop; male wage. Number of observations on common support are 742.

Table 6.3 Regression adjusted matching estimates of training impact on assets and income by training provider ($\times 10^{-2}$)

Matching algorithm	Training by NGOs		Training by government	
	(1) Gross assets	*(2) Income*	*(3) Gross assets*	*(4) Income*
LLR (bw 1) (S.E.)	387.1***	18.75	−469.07	66.96 (7,032)
	(11,002)	(1,366)	(37,314)	
LLR (bw 4) (S.E.)	387.1***	18.75	−469.07	66.96 (6,619)
	(12,639)	(1,459)	(36,047)	

Source: Bali Swain and Varghese 2010b.

Notes
** Significant at the 5% level. * Significant at the 10% level. LLR = local linear regression, *p*-values in parentheses standard errors created by bootstrap replications of 200.
a Covariates of regression same at Table 2, (5) and (6), omitting the training variable. See text for definition of variables. Number of observations on common support are 742.

training one finds a strong impact on assets. Training organized by government officials does not show any impact. To check robustness of these results Bali Swain and Varghese (2011b) conducted sensitivity analyses of their results to unobservables (Ichino *et al.* 2007). They find that their results are robust.

In sum, with regression adjusted matching results (which correct for both training and membership endogeneity) one finds a strong impact overall on assets but not on income. Furthermore, infrastructure and organizers of training matter in that they positively impact training delivery.

Investigating the impact of the level of infrastructure and business training, Bali Swain and Varghese (2010b) find that training has a much higher impact on assets when made available to SHGs in villages closest to paved roads. For effective training impact on assets, the location of the village matters and households benefit from better market connectivity. Using SIAS data their results show that for those receiving training, assets can drop by about Rs.5,000 for every kilometre of distance from a paved road. With income generation, again one does not observe a similar impact, possibly due to the fact that households may consume their own products without relying on the market.

Correcting for endogeniety, their regression adjusted matching estimates show an even stronger impact on assets but none on income suggesting that those receiving training had greater income beforehand. Their results indicate that infrastructure matters, as members located in villages closer to paved roads benefit with a positive impact on assets with training.

Type of training

Given the involvement of heterogeneous SHPIs with their own development agenda, the SHGs have been exposed to different types of training programmes. These included a range of programmes focusing on occupational skill development, marketing, healthcare training, literacy and family planning, etc. Obviously, not all these training programmes were aimed towards direct impact on income generation. Bali Swain and Varghese (2010b) term skill development and marketing training as business training and investigate their impact on assets and income. Their analysis shows that business training has a stronger significant impact on assets but not on income. Thus, business training and participation can have immediate effects on asset accumulation but translating these into income is problematic for MFIs.

Turning to investigate this further by breakdown by linkage model, their results show that only when NGOs specialize in training and banks in lending (the more popular linkage model 2) does business training have a strongly positive significant impact on assets.

Computing a crude measure of returns on assets by examining the point estimates they find a return of 18 per cent of basic training. With more specialized training such as business training, these returns may be increased to 23 per cent (Bali Swain and Varghese 2010b). Finally, with business training and linkage model 2, these returns increase to 34 per cent.

The conditional independence assumption which propensity score matching rests on is untestable, but testing their results they find them robust to two different observables (young and education) that mimic the unobservables.

Concluding discussion

This chapter evaluated the impact of training in Self Help Groups on two outcome measures, income and assets. Using regression adjusted matching methods, the recent research shows that training impacts assets and not income. These results resonate with parallel work where one finds that membership positively impacts asset creation and not income. The impact of training on assets reveals that training strengthens members' skills in savings and asset accumulation. The lack of impact on income indicates that much more needs to be established for training to have a positive discernible impact on income generation. For instance, marketable goods, infrastructure and other factors play an important role and, paradoxically, the effects on income generation may take more time than asset accumulation.

In terms of the data used, even though the SIAS data provides superior information on training for SHGs as compared to other data sets, more work needs to be done on data collection. The measure of quantity of training in SIAS is provided in weeks. A finer measure such as hours of training may provide different results. Furthermore, a better distinction of the types of training programmes would also help in differentiating the ones that had most impact. Future work should examine the relationship between softer skills of training such as education and its impact on other outcome measures such as schooling. Though this type of training may incur costs now, it has future payoffs.

In terms of implementation, according to NCAER (2008), more than 80 per cent of SHGs face problems in developing the skills of their members. Major reasons cited were lack of time, lack of interest, inadequate literacy among the members and insufficient training facilities. In their survey the SHGs in all the states suggested that the SHPIs allow more time in training and group discussions. They further required support from financial institutions in training on book keeping, reviewing and advice on SHG financial activities and health. Furthermore, the NCAER (2008) study argues that since training programmes are not homogenized and they vary by NGOs, it becomes difficult to grade the quality of the training programme.

Two recent implementations offer directions for future improvements in the training programmes. Nussbaum *et al.* (2005), in a recent microenterprise study, questioned the trainers that were employed by the SHGs to provide feedback on how the training programme could be improved. These same trainers were then asked to conduct training programmes based on their insights. The recipients of this training perceived the improved programmes as much higher quality. Another programme initiated by the SBLP is the Microenterprise Development Programme (MEDP) which began in 2006. This training programme targets skill development for mature SHGs. Here, the initial demand for skill training comes from the SHGs and the SHPIs apply for grants to impart the relevant skill training. Another appealing aspect of this programme is that the length of the training is limited to two weeks and can also be a minimum of three days.

In general, training provided under the SBLP has a positive impact on assets. The quantity of training in weeks does not make any difference to either assets or income. Good village infrastructure helps training's effectiveness in asset accumulation. When NGOs help form SHGs and banks finance groups, training has the greatest impact on income.

In conclusion, the empirical evidence presented in this chapter has some programmatic lessons. Linkages between banks (even public sector ones) and NGOs may provide effective means for credit delivery. The results thus support the expansion of these types of linkage and suggest avoiding the use of government officials as training organizers in the SBLP.

7 Achieving impact and meeting challenges

Introduction

The Indian government remains committed to SBLP, which is considered a major strategy for poverty alleviation and gender empowerment. In his Union Budget speech of 2011–12, India's finance minister, Pranab Mukherjee stated that Micro Finance Institutions (MFIs) had emerged as an important means to financial inclusion. For providing equity to smaller MFIs, he proposed the 'India Microfinance Equity Fund' of Rs.1 billion with SIDBI. The minister also stated that to empower women and promote their Self Help Groups (SHGs), he intended to create a 'Women's SHG's Development Fund' with a corpus of Rs.5 billion.[1] Given the Indian government's confidence in the programme and the magnitude of resources invested in SBLP, it is worthwhile to investigate the extent of SBLP impact on the member households, typically in women's and economic empowerment.

Investigating two important dimensions of well-being, Chapter 3 investigated whether the SBLP impact reduces poverty and vulnerability. Defining vulnerability as a forward-looking, *ex-ante* measure of the household's ability to cope with future shocks and proneness to food insecurity, empirical analysis was conducted using SIAS data. Exploring the programme's impact on vulnerability, it was found that the household's ability to mitigate risk and cope with shocks is enhanced through SHG participation by increasing household earnings through provision of microfinance and training, aiding the household in the face of shocks by providing consumption loans, and enhancing their resilience by strengthening social support and improving women's empowerment.

Even though SHG-member households are found to be poorer than the non-SHG member (control group) households, they are not more vulnerable. Vulnerability is significantly lower for the more mature households as compared to the non-SHG members. Favourable initial conditions and enabling socio-economic environment, like better infrastructure, assist SHGs to be more effective in reducing vulnerability. Contrary to expectations the type of linkage where the SHG is both financed and formed by the banks seem to be the most effective in reducing vulnerability.

The flexibility of a joint liability microfinance programme like SBLP permits the loan to be used for any purpose, production or consumption. SBLP thereby provides the participating households with the possibility for consumption smoothing, thus reducing the variability in food consumption levels and hence vulnerability. It strengthens mutual support networks that help reduce vulnerability of members and that of their households in ways that may not be adequately captured by the change in household earnings. These empirical results have important implications for the SHG programme, where policy makers may maximize the impact of SHG through provision of better infrastructural facilities and using the linkage model 2 where NGOs form the SHGs and banks provide them with finance.

Chapter 4 examined whether SHG participation has long-term impact on member households through asset creation and whether it impacts parameters such as income. This is important since assets underlie the structural determinant of poverty. The evidence presented in this chapter shows that longer membership duration in SHGs positively impacts asset creation. These results are robust to various specifications of assets. However, there was no evidence for impact on short-term variables such as total current income. The impact on asset accumulation arises from the savings requirement in the programme and livestock accumulation which then leads to income diversification. The type of SHG linkage model is found to have no effect.

These conclusions imply that the linkages between banks and NGOs may provide effective means for credit delivery. This chapter reveals that in terms of impact on asset accumulation, linkage 3 (where the funding is channelled through NGOs) is the most effective. To a certain extent the recent explosion of MFIs in the SBLP and their exponential growth may be a positive development in this regard. Through group savings and training, SBLP creates asset accumulation and can contribute positively towards income generation through further diversification into non-farm activities.

Defining women empowerment within the South Asian context, an empirical analysis was conducted to evaluate the impact of SBLP in empowering women in Chapter 5. The results strongly demonstrate that on average, there is a significant increase in the empowerment of the women participants. This, however, does not mean that all members are empowered, or that they are empowered in the same degree or/and at the same pace. The economic impact of SBLP is found to empower women most. However, greater autonomy and changes in social attitudes are also important in empowering women. The SBLP should continue to place a greater emphasis on training, education of women and creating awareness, with increased investment in social intermediation. Without these, channelling microfinance through women's groups alone might result in several other positive outcomes but may not translate into a sustainable long-term impact in empowering women.

Chapter 6 evaluated whether the impact of 'microfinance plus', or the disbursement of services beyond credit, amplifies the impact of SBLP. The investigation reveals that training has a definite positive impact on assets but not on income. The impact of training can be improved through better infrastructure (as in paved roads), linkage model type and the training organizer. Provision of business training with SBLP microfinance leads to a larger positive impact on assets for the participating households. Again, these results advocate that linkages between banks and NGOs may provide effective means for credit delivery. However, the use of government officials as training organizers in the SBLP should be avoided. The overtly positive impact of the SBLP programme presented here needs to be balanced with some of the critical challenges that it faces.

Critical challenges for SBLP

With the lack of initial enthusiasm and motivated human resources at NABARD and the NGOs in the field, the SBLP has lost its early thrust. The entry of government agencies and contracted staff has led to an increasing concern about the SBLP as the programme's growth has been unable to keep pace with its capacity to ensure quality. Ghate *et al.* (2007) points out that while slower growth will not in itself resolve the problem, there is a need to expand the programmes in the slower growing central and eastern regions of India. The expansion of the programme in the 13 priority states is relying on the relatively weak government promoted groups due to the lack of quality NGOs at the grassroots level. He further notes that greater depth of outreach (in terms of higher proportion of clients under the poverty line), better book-keeping capacity and maintaining improved performance in terms of lower dropout rates, greater equity of loan distribution within groups and promoting their longevity remains vital.

Basu (2006) agrees that some of the main challenges facing SHGs are the inadequate attention to group quality, capacity constraints and cost of group formation. Srinivasan (2010) notes that the SBLP is stagnating with the credit disbursal in 2010 around the same levels as 2009. Linkage of newly formed groups to banks is slow and there seems to be a general credit linkage fatigue setting in the banks. Taking stock of the SBLP, this section discusses some of the critical challenges faced by this programme: challenges that it needs to meet, if the SBLP is to expand to the next level.

Outreach and sustainability

Based on the evidence presented in this book it is clear that microfinance has the potential to reduce poverty and vulnerability, but if inclusion of the poor decreases, there will be a definite dilution of the impact. Sinha *et al.* (2009) based on their sample suggest that over half of the SHG members are below the Indian poverty line (with a similar proportion of poor for those who have been SHG members for seven years). They also find a substantial representation of the structurally poor (scheduled tribe (ST), schedule caste (SC) and women heads of households), even though SHG leaders tend to be better off than the average member, with some schooling. Overall they find that illiteracy is high and has a negative impact on the ability of record-keeping and accounting in SHGs.

This is supported by Basu (2006), who finds that in Andhra Pradesh (south) and Uttar Pradesh (north) nearly 54 per cent of the SHG members are from the poorest groups – landless and marginal farmers. Using various household attributes they also show that SHGs are quite effective in targeting poorer households.

Harper (Fisher *et al.* 2002), however, argues that the evidence shows that SHGs are probably less likely to include poorest. However SHGs provide a broader range of services and greater flexibility of members in choosing which services to access, and thus may be more suitable for poorer people. He further notes that SHGs are a more empowering instrument than Grameen groups but they are also more demanding of their members, and expose them to greater risks.

Mahajan (2007) objects to the assumption that the poor all wish to be self-employed and can be helped by microcredit. He argues that the majority of the poor people, particularly the poorest (such as landless labourers in India) want steady wage-employment, on- or off-farm. Quoting Hulme and Mosley (1969), Mahajan argues that the increase in income of microcredit borrowers is directly proportional to their starting level of income – the poorer they were to start with, the lower is the impact of the loan. He points out that the not so poor also lack access to credit and have an equally important need for it, arguing further that it is not the not so poor who generate wage employment opportunities for the poorest, and enable microcredit to spread its costs over a larger clientele.

Seibel (2001) suggests that the SHG system is unsustainable, due to lack of clarity on who maintains the quality and how these costs are being met. Especially in the long run it is uncertain as to who will finance and monitor the groups. Seibel suggests that the NGOs with their socio-development perspectives might not be the ideal candidate to do this.

Mahajan (2007) argues that it takes too long to be sustainable, perhaps even early subsidies are required. For instance, the SHG programme provides external support to the one-time costs of group formation and ongoing group support costs. With increased political pressure to lower interest rates on loans to SHGs or provide subsidized interest rates, even the variable costs are not being met in most places according to Mahajan.

On the contrary, taking the case study of Rudrapur, Harper (2002) tentatively concludes that the SHG system is more economical and thus financially sustainable, in the short to medium term, although he agrees that capturing of the SHGs through government programmes like the SGSY have polluted the groups through subsidy.

Concentration of microfinance in the three southern states of Andhra Pradesh, Tamil Nadu and Karnataka seems to be a continuing concern. In Andhra, for instance, there are 9.63 microloans for every poor household and three microloans for every two households in the state (Srinivasan 2010). The State Credit Plan allocated 24 per cent of credit for SHG lending in Andhra Pradesh, which is the largest support to any types of community based groups in the country (Srinivasan 2010).

Sinha *et al.* (2009) note that Andhra Pradesh, Tamil Nadu, Karnataka and Kerala account for 54 per cent of the SHGs and 75 per cent of SHG bank credit even though they constitute only 20 per cent of the population. This is predominantly due to historically stronger NGOs in the south. Overcoming the concentration in the southern states is important. Mahajan and Gupta (2003) agree that the central, eastern and north-eastern economies in India have been relatively left behind, resulting in limited demand for credit, especially amongst the subsistence poor. They suggest that lack of good quality NGOs have been an added factor.

The rapid growth of the microfinance industry in south India was hit by a crisis that had been brewing up for some time, erupting in the form of a spate of suicides by microfinance borrowers in Andhra Pradesh due to overindebtedness, around September and October 2010. Multiple borrowing, default crisis, high interest rates and coercive recovery of loans were cited as the main reasons by the media. Following public uproar, the Andhra Pradesh state government brought in an ordinance on 14 October 2010, making it compulsory for MFIs to register themselves, declare the effective interest rate that they were charging and ensure that no security was sought for loans and no coercion was used for recovery. Non-compliance was punishable with a three-year prison term and a fine of Rs.100,000 (*The Telegraph*, 19 October 2010).

According to Johnson and Meka (2010), about 93 per cent of all households in Andhra Pradesh had access to loans. Of these 37.5 per cent were from formal institutions, 53 per cent from SHGs and 11 per cent from MFIs. Borrowings from informal sources (friends and relatives) accounted for 82 (74) per cent of the total loans. The median number of loans per households was four, and 83 per cent of the families had two or more loans. With the increase in multiple borrowing, the average loan size was also increasing. This combined with the heterogenous groups induced an increase in default rate. Johnson and Meka (2010) also found that in Andhra Pradesh the number of SHG borrowers were five times more than those who borrowed from an MFI. Moreover, 67 per cent of the MFI borrowers had also borrowed from an SHG.

With increasing saturation in targeted markets, the competition amongst the MFIs intensified. Availability of loans from several institutions (MFIs and SHGs) and increased pressure on the MFI staff to achieve targets and break even within short periods, led to multiple borrowings and, in some cases, excessive debt (Srinivasan 2010). Excesses in the form of high interest rates being charged and coercive loan practices by some MFIs were widely reported in the media and induced the state governments in south India (Andhra Pradesh, Tamil Nadu, Kerala) to use law and administrative controls on the MFIs. This rapid expansion of microfinance in south India also raises important issues related to the interest rates charged, excessive debt, coercive recovery practices and some form of regulation and quality control.

Capacity constraints and the cost of group formation

The estimated cost of creating and sustaining new and high quality SHGs varies. NABARD claims that it is about Rs.1,000 per group, whereas some NGOs suggest about Rs.12,000. The NCAER (2008) study puts the promotional cost[2] of SHGs at Rs.4,045 for NGOs, at Rs.3,562 for governments and at Rs.2,440 for banks, in 2004. The Ministry of Rural Development, Government of India, has established a norm of Rs.10,000 per group. NCAER (2008) also documents the additional maintenance costs such as training, book-keeping, social mobilization, for stability and sustainability of SHGs. They find that the maintenance cost by a SHPI is often less than the funds deployed to promote it. The banks spend Rs.964 per SHG towards maintenance, whereas a non-bank SHPI incurred Rs.1,123 per SHG in 2005. In addition, NCAER (2008) finds that to promote and monitor new SHGS, the SHPIs received support for financing and promoting the SHGs from NABARD and banks. About 28 per cent of the SHPIs were state government supported.

According to Basu (2006) state-owned banks have been lending to SHGs at interest rates of between 9 per cent and 12 per cent per year, as compared to other studies that impute the value at 15 per cent to 28 per cent per year. Unless banks are able to charge the interest rates that enable them to recover costs, the model's financial viability and longer-term sustainability will remain difficult. Harper (2002) notes that the loans to SHGs were excluded from the maximum interest ceiling of 12 per cent that still applies to other loans under Rs.20,000 (RBI 2000), but banks are not charging higher interest rates. According to Harper, given the higher repayment rates a net difference of 5.5 per cent in the interest rate is enough to cover their transaction costs, as long as the task of promoting, training and developing SHGs is carried out by an NGO, at no cost to the bank.

In July 2010, the RBI removed the ceiling on the interest rates on small loans and allowed the banks to charge a service fee to customers on loans that was serviced through the business correspondents (BCs). This was done with the intention to encourage and provide the banks with alternative promoting agents (BCs) to reach the microfinance clients directly instead of providing bulk loans to MFIs.

Savings

Discussing the usurious moneylender, Bhaduri (1977) argued that for the poor, saving is not possible as they are too close to subsistence. Thus, they require credit not savings. Subsidized banking across the developing world remained focused on lending at a subsidized interest rate instead of focusing on savings; this was misinterpreted by many to suggest that the poor lacked the ability rather than the opportunity to save (Adams 1984). Arguing further, Adams and von Pischke (1992) suggest that savings, not loans, are more critical for the poorest whereas the relatively better off may be a more suitable target for loans. Armendáriz and Morduch (2010) with their middle view suggest that the very poor need both savings and borrowing.

Studying consumption smoothing behaviour of households, Deaton (1992) shows that effective and active consumption smoothing may be achieved with low levels of average assets. He argues that households that face recurrent shocks are more eager to save.

Acting as self-insurance, savings absorb the small shocks to the household, like illness, etc. Faced with vulnerability and livelihood risks, insurance also becomes important, for instance crop insurance or insurance of income earning assets like livestock. Involuntary or compulsory micro-savings programmes help the clients build up assets over time and develop the discipline of saving. However, some argue that compulsory savings is a way for MFIs to acquire cheap capital and secure a form of (financial) collateral from borrowers, since the savings may be confiscated in case of default or the member leaving the group.

One of the main strengths of the SHG programme is the primary focus on savings. However, Isern *et al.* (2007) find that some group members do not use SHGs for savings. According to them SHGs mobilize only modest amounts of member savings, mainly through compulsory deposits that members make, not because they want to save, but only because the deposits are required to get a loan. Few SHGs offer voluntary savings, possibly because they involve complexities such as liquidity management, more staff or volunteer time to meet member requests for access to their savings, and more record-keeping for SHG managers. This could be partly related to the literacy constraints of the SHGs and the legal restrictions on organizations to provide the opportunity to save. It is critical to find an effective way to ensure the performance and quality of the savings and credit group.

Flexible products

In terms of evaluating the effectiveness of Indian SHGs Isern *et al.* (2007) find that the Indian SHGs are effective in reaching the vulnerable and marginalized groups. Their study shows that though SHGs reach poor and excluded groups, their financial services are not fully matched to the member needs. According to the Center for Microfinance study (CMF 2010) on SHGs in Andhra Pradesh, SHG loans form only 5.4 per cent of the total borrowings of members, with 75.4 per cent loans borrowed from informal sources and 17.8 per cent directly from the banks.

Basu (2006) also points that India's rural poor need to meet their diverse financial needs (savings credit, insurance, etc.) through varied, more flexible products at competitive prices. In addition to introducing flexible products, there is a need for composite financial services (including lending, savings and insurance). Banking procedures, like opening a bank account and accessing credit, require simplification and well-trained personnel who understand clients' needs with a focus on doorstep banking. Using technology (smart cards, biometrics) that reduce the transaction costs further could also be experimented with. While agreeing that microfinance can deliver loans effectively, Basu suggests that medium-term strategy should be to graduate clients to the formal financial system.

Morduch and Rutherford (2003) argue that the SHG lacks a system of moving the SHG members towards individual loans on a more commercial basis and there exist a limited number of lenders that these borrowers may graduate to. They also suggest that institutions like regional rural banks need to be reformed and design services and products that are appropriate for the SHG clients.

Quality of SHG groups

Over the years there has been a symptotic increase in the SBLP default rate that reflects some of the above discussed problems, and also a decline in group quality. According to Srinivasan (2009), about 2.9 per cent of the total outstanding loans to the SHGs were defaulted loans. At the disaggregated level, 2.1 per cent of commercial banks, 4.5 per cent of RRBs and 4.8 per cent of cooperative banks' outstanding loans were defaulted on for the financial year that ended March 2008. Only 46.5 per cent of the banks had recoveries of more than 95 per cent. Eighteen of the 33 public and private sector commercial banks had a recovery rate of 95 per cent and above. However, six banks have recoveries between 80 and 94 per cent, whereas eight of them had recoveries between 50 and 79 per cent. Geographically, Uttar Pradesh reported the highest non-performing assets (Srinivasan 2009). The quality of the groups have been affected by high levels of defaults. This is evident in Andhra Pradesh where recovery rates are between 80 and 85 per cent. The default rates are higher for SGSY. Even when the SHGs do not default, repayment rates on internal loans within the groups are very low, at 35 per cent to 40 per cent (Srinivasan 2010).

According to the NCAER (2008) study 48 per cent of the SHPIs reported illiteracy and people's ignorance regarding the benefits of SHGs as major problems in promoting new SHGs. About 28 per cent reported constraints from shortage of field staff, while 24 per cent indicated lack of financial support as one of the major problems in promoting new SHGs. Regarding linking SHGs to banks, 45 per cent of the SHPIs faced difficulties due to lack of interest from SHG members, 41 per cent revealed lack of cooperation from the bank managers, irregular visits by them and frequent postponement of date for providing loans.

In his interview, the Branch Manager in Warangal[3] suggested that the SBLP was constrained by illiteracy that not only inhibited the socio-economic development but also limited the ability of the group to maintain their accounts. The groups had a limited capacity to absorb credit, thus preventing the bankers to sanction larger loans. The rotation of leadership was also limited within the groups, due to lack of second line leadership and educated members. SHGs were also spread thin over various responsibilities such as implementing the midday meal scheme in village schools, running fair price shops, etc.

Basu (2006) suggests that according to leading NGOs engaged in SBLP, it takes a minimum of three years of nurturing before a group is ready to be linked to a bank. However, banks and government officials might not have the interest and time to get involved in book-keeping of the groups' internal savings and loan accounts. The group quality is thus negatively affected.

Moreover, government programmes like SGSY scheme include a subsidy component which may further corrupt the borrower's interest to repay, thus impacting the SHG group quality. Subsidized loans to one group may also lead to envy of other SHGs that may not be eligible for a similar subsidized loan. In an interview, a banker from Rae Bareli, Uttar Pradesh,[4] argued that the provision of the subsidy to SHG under SGSY was demotivating other groups.

The interview with the Bank Manager from Gadchiroli[5] clearly quantified the reasons for which the SHG programmes might face a problematic situation due to the SGSY and other government programmes. He suggested that the target oriented schemes of the SGSY were not provided according to the group's needs and therefore there was a greater scope of misuse of these loans. Explaining this further a government official[6] argued that there was a mismatch between the requirement of the SHG members and the government programme. For instance, if the member's loan requirement is only Rs.100, then providing him/her with Rs.1,000 might lead to problems as he/she might not have the capacity to manage or absorb it.

The government programmes with subsidized loans do not have an encouraging history in India. Integrated Rural Development Programme (IRDP), which was one of the largest anti-poverty programmes implemented in India, had bank loans as a major component. These loans had repayment rates of 40 per cent and less. By adopting the SHGs, SGSY provides capital and interest subsidy for investment loans. As opposed to SHG-based microfinance programmes, SGSY lending by banks is mandatory. However, as opposed to IRDP, under SGSY, a major component of grants and loans are provided to SHGs rather than individuals. SGSY envisages an increased role for banks, NGOs and government-owned District Development Agencies that are the primary implementing agencies. However, such agencies lack the required capacity to administer such programmes, a situation that has been made worse by increasing pressure on the village and block level administrators to achieve targets on creation of SHGs (Nair 2005).

Ghate *et al.* (2007) agrees that groups promoted by the field level government officials who are given targets in addition to regular duties tend to be the weakest, as they have a very low capacity to support the groups after they have been formed. The SGSY is being transformed into an integrated livelihood development intervention, named the National Rural Livelihoods Mission (NRLM) and exactly how the NRLM will be implemented is yet to be studied.

An added concern was that outsiders like politicians were interfering in the working of the SHGs.[7] Hinting at some emerging problems, the Medak district's AGM of NABARD also mentioned that the SHG leaders had become very influential in the villages. With the private sector, approaching the SHGs as their delivery or marketing agents. There was a greater need for the SHGs' sensitization to the corporate sector.[8]

Politicians view the SBLP programme as a vote winner, thereby pushing for quantitative targets that do not control for group quality. Some groups are put together in an ad hoc manner without proper quality control and may threaten the longer-term credibility and viability of the entire programme (Basu 2006).

In recent years the Panchayats (local governments) have also become involved in promoting SHGs and are giving competition to NGOs and rural banks in forming SHGs. However, the quality of SHGs formed by Panchayats is inferior to those formed by NGOs. Panchayats have been also criticized on the grounds that they influence who receives government subsidy, that they are open to political pressure and that funds are misused by the recommending Panchayats and/or political parties.

Households borrow from SHGs and MFIs, and informal sources. However, with the recent aggressive growth of MFIs in the Indian microfinance sector, especially in Southern India, there is an overlap of about 10 per cent between the SHGs and the MFIs. The overlap between MFIs is much higher, with multiple loans in competitive locations resulting in a customer to accounts ratio of 2:3 (Srinivasan 2010). The default rates of SHGs are also increasing (Srinivasan 2010). The mass default problem in Kolar, where borrowers were incited to default on religious grounds, has also ignited fears and made the MFIs wary of expanding microfinance in certain regions and to certain communities.

Loans were forgiven prior to elections due to the pressure on the state banks, this led to further problems by removing incentives for management to build tight institutions. The waivers of farm sector loans and multiple lending under MFIs have also had a negative impact on repayment (Srinivasan 2009).

In our field interviews, several bankers noted that SBLP provide the government and bankers with a delivery mechanism through which several central and state poverty alleviation programmes and loans can be delivered through a simple and easy process. However, the Lead District Manager from Villupuram,[9] Tamil Nadu in his interview cautioned that with several governments, banks and NGOs using SHGs as a delivery mechanism to deliver services or achieve targets, the SBLP is like a bubble that might burst under the strain from all these programmes. For instance, at the time of the interview in Villupuram, Tamil Nadu, SHGs were used to deliver the Tamil Nadu Adi-Dravidar Housing and Development Corporation (THADCO), Training of Rural Youth for Self Employment (TRYSEM) and Swarnajayanti Gram Swarozgar Yojana (SGSY).

Overloading SBLP

Microfinance is a means or instrument of development, not an end in itself. With its initial phenomenal success many perceive that the microcredit movement has made the assumption that credit is the main financial service needed by the poor, whereas the poor need and want to save.

Others believe that credit can automatically translate into successful microenterprises. Mahajan (2007) argues that microcredit is a necessary but not a sufficient condition for microenterprise development. As argued in Chapter 6, he explains that, like identification of livelihood opportunities, selection and motivation of the micro-entrepreneurs, it is also important to provide business and technical training, establish market linkages for inputs and outputs and common infrastructure and time regulatory approvals. Without these microcredit works only for a limited set of activities – small farming, livestock rearing and petty trading, etc. Only 11.7 per cent of the SHG loans were starting a new business or for trading or investing in livestock (Srinivasan 2010).

Regulation

Government needs to make key reforms to improve the overall incentive framework, as well as the regulatory and legal system within which rural banks operate, so as to promote greater efficiency and competition in rural finance.

While the RRBs and rural cooperative banks need restructuring (as supported by various government committees), with greater supervision and prudential regulation standards related to capital adequacy, asset classification, income recognition and provisioning need to be upgraded and introduced in a phased manner, and supervisory enforcement improved. Basu (2006) also suggests that the weaknesses in regulatory standards, poor enforcement and regulatory tolerance that have undermined market discipline and contributed to the deep financial distress that characterizes many RRBs and cooperatives.

Indian microfinance is different from microfinance in other parts of the world as the microfinance institutions in India are not allowed to mobilize savings (Ghate *et al*. 2007). The Microfinance Regulation Bill was introduced with the aim to promote and regulate the microfinance sector and permit microfinance organizations to collect deposits from eligible clients. The bill is expected to bring the microfinance sector in India under the surveillance of NABARD. The proposed bill is still waiting to be voted in the parliament to become law.

Concluding remarks

Unlike other development programmes, Seibel (2006) emphasizes that SHG banking has emerged from the Indian agencies and organizations, driven by ownership at all institutional levels from SHGs with their federations, up to NABARD and RBI. The SBLP fits very well with the strong commitment in India to democratic organization and decentralization. By building on the existing rural financial infrastructure of a large network of rural bank branches and non-government organizations, it has erected a sustainable structure of support for the SBLP.

The SBLP is now almost two decades old. Piloted in 1992, it has grown, evolved and matured over the years. While the multi-dimensional impact evidence of SBLP presented in this book allows us to be optimistic about this programme, we are also at the threshold of addressing some of the long-standing challenges.

Appendix 1

Profile of selected districts by states

The information in this section is based on field interviews conducted at the district level with NABARD officials, participating bankers and government officials and partners.

Andhra Pradesh

Andhra Pradesh ranks first in the country in terms of the formation and linkage of SHGs with banks. At the time of the survey almost 50 per cent of the total Indian SHGs were from Andhra. According to the Microcredit Innovations Department (Mcid) Deputy General Manager (DGM) in NABARD's Regional Office at Hyderabad[1] there were more than 400,000 SHGs existing in Andhra Pradesh, of which 281,000 SHGs had been linked to formal financial institutions like banks. Many SHGs were transformed groups that were initially formed under the Development of Women and Child in Rural Areas (DWCRA) programme. The SHG programme gained momentum in the state during 1995–96. The District Rural Development Agency (DRDA) of Andhra Pradesh played the main role in formation of SHGs, their capacity building and linkage with banks. The DRDA was headed by a Project Director who was supported by four Assistant Project officers, an Extension Officer (DWCRA) and Community Coordinators under the state's Velugu programme. The effort was also supported by other NGOs and banks. SHG federations and Mutually Aided Cooperative Societies (MACS) were also established by 2003.

The Andhra government has been very active within the state in formation, linkage and use of SHGs as a delivery mechanism. Gram Deepikas were selected by SHG members and appointed by the state government to maintain SHG records, coordinate with banks/government agencies and nurture the SHGs. Gram Deepika is a person at the village level appointed to take up the responsibility of capacity building of SHGs and co-ordination with external agencies. On average they were accountable to about 20 SHGs. Part of their salary was paid by the SHGs and part by the government in the form of providing them a priority status in their selection into schemes like Deepam Patnagam (a scheme for obtaining cooking gas connection) and Grihini (a housing scheme) which involves subsidy. In comparison to other states the scale is much higher in Andhra because it was a banker driven programme. Having tasted success in the initial phase the bankers have been willing to take the SBLP to a higher level. Also, with the emergence of MACS and SHG federations the scale of lending and saving has increased many times over. SHGs in Andhra have taken up activities like dairy, animal husbandry, vegetable cultivation and processing and marketing of spices. For instance, Rudramaa milk is marked by SHG groups in Jangaon Mandal of Warangal district.

The selected survey districts of Warangal and Medak provide a fair representation of the SHG programme within the state. Medak district is economically poor and drought prone. The SBLP has been instrumental in prevention of migration and distress selling of assets and financial exploitation. In both the districts MACS structure are taking shape. In Warangal MACS have started marketing of toned milk and spices, coir-based activities have also been taken up by SHGs on a large scale.

The Medak district DDM of NABARD provided the following information about the district. At the time of survey, about 17,000 SHGs had been formed in Medak district, of which 15,000 were operational while 2,000 lay dormant. The DRDA was the main agency participating in SHG formation. NGOs also played a crucial role in SHG formation and capacity building. Among NGOs Navajyothi and the Society for Women Awareness and Rural Development (SWARD) had participated actively. In 2003, the SHGs joined to form federations and Mutually Aided Cooperative Societies.

The District Development Manager (DDM, NABARD) in Warangal district disclosed that the state government was very active in SHG formation and linkage of SHGs with banks in the district. About 1,100 Gram Deepikas had been appointed by the state government (one per village) during the time of the survey.

Maharashtra

During 2003, Maharashtra was ranked seventh in the country for its SBLP. Within the state the selected districts of Chandrapur and Gadchiroli had the first and third largest numbers of SHGs in the state of Maharashtra during the time of the survey. As reported in an interview by Mr M.I. Ganagi[2] the salient characteristic of SHGs in these two districts was the absence of mixed groups, and the groups were also fairly homogeneous with their members belonging to the same class. According to Gadchiroli's District General Manager,[3] the recovery from SHGs was almost 100 per cent. The SHG members were small or marginal farmers, landless labourers and rural women. There was no overlap in the population targeted by the formal credit programmes of banks and their SHG programmes in the district. The SBLP targeted rural women who had no previous link to the banks but were now eligible to be linked with banks for formal credits through the SHG programme.

Chandrapur district[4]

The geographical area of Chandrapur district is 1.1 million hectares, of which almost half is occupied by forest. The gross cropped area was 0.5 million hectares. The district has five major perennial rivers, which offer a large potential for promotion of a lift irrigation scheme.

The economy of the district is largely agriculture based. A vast majority of the rural population depends for their livelihood on farm and off-farm activities. At the time of the survey the population of the district was about 2.1 million with a rural population of 71 per cent.

Chandrapur district is a backward district with a substantial tribal population (about 20 per cent). The district has a few key industries like coal, cement, paper, megathermal power station, refrigeration and chemical units. At the time of the survey Chandrapur had a total of 232 bank branches of various banking agencies, consisting of 109 commercial banks, 40 RRBs, and 71 DCCBs. The network spread of banks and financial institutions was considered adequate to effectively take care of the financial services in the district.

Tamil Nadu

The state ranks second in terms of the SHG–Bank Linkage Programme after Andhra Pradesh. The SBLP commenced in Tamil Nadu right from the introduction of the Pilot Project for linking 500 SHGs to banks in 1991–92. A modest beginning of linking 22 SHGs was made then and as on 31 March 2003, around 99,184 SHGs had been credit linked in Tamil Nadu and the Union Territory of Pondicherry. The Tamil Nadu Corporation for the Development of Women (TNCDW) has also played a vital role in implementing the SHG Linkage Programme in the state. TNCDW was set up by the state government of Tamil Nadu to promote women SHGs in the state. The TNCDW forms and promotes SHGs and thereafter covers them under SGSY. The expansion of the SBLP in the state has been made easier due to the large number of NGOs that have been active in forming and linking the SHGs.

Of the linkage models, the second model (banks promoting SHGs through NGOs) was the most effective in the state during the time of the survey. The quality of SHGS formed in the state is fairly good. The salient characteristic of SHGs in the state is the same as in respect of any other state. The selected districts for the survey in Tamil Nadu were Dharmapuri and Villupuram. The SHGs in Dharmapuri were inclined towards farm sector activities, whereas the Villupuram SHGs were engaged in non-farm sector activities.

The interview with the DDM of Dharmapuri[5] revealed that at the time of the survey the district already had about 12,000 formed SHGs. Among these 10,613 SHGs had been linked with banks. The NGOs were engaged in intermediation between the bank and government. There were 19 commercial banks and 127 branches, one RRB with 25 branches, and one DCCB with 39 branches in the district at the time of the survey. About 31 NGOs were operating in the district for promoting SHGs. Much importance was given to the group formation stage where factors such as homogeneity, sustained savings and democratic functioning were emphasized. In Dharmapuri district 2,423 SHGs had been linked as of March 2002, and about 4,500 SHGs were linked during 2003.

The NABARD AGM[6] explained that the Villupuram district was amongst the top two SHG districts in the state and the SBLP was working smoothly in the district. The bankers, District Collector TNCDW had extended the state financed Tamil Nadu women's development project 'Bangaru Ammaiar Ninaivu Mahalir Thittam', to be implemented in all of the 22 blocks of the district from 1998. The objective of the project was the development of strong and cohesive women SHGs, promotion of saving habits, improved access to various government development schemes and bank welfare schemes, development of leadership qualities and improved status of women in the family and the society. According to the evaluations, the programme was working successfully in the district. In addition, the government adopted all poverty alleviation programmes like the SGSY through the SBLP.

Uttar Pradesh

Compared to other Indian states, Uttar Pradesh was relatively slow in developing the SBLP. The selected districts of Allahabad and Rae Bareli were top-performing within the SBLP but average districts within the state. According to their mission objective, NABARD should reach about 80 per cent of the rural poor population, but by 31 March 2003 they had reached only about 48 per cent of the population.

The MCID DDM from NABARD's regional office in Lucknow[7] further confirmed that the state government was not very active in promoting the SBLP. Mostly the SGSY functioned through the SHGs. The government programmes were target oriented and were not successful for the SBLP.

NABARD's DDM in Rae Bareli in Uttar Pradesh[8] reported that all 15 blocks in the district were credit linked. The total number of bank branches in the district were 154 (with 55 commercial banks, 69 RRBs and 30 DCCBs). Of these 111 (26 commercial banks, 69 RRBs and 16 DCCBs) were participating in the SBLP. The number of savings linked SHGs was 5,070, whereas the credit linked SHGs were 2,503, as on 31 August 2003. SHGs were initially formed in the district in 1994 by Uttar Pradesh Bhumi Sudhar Nigam in the villages, which was implemented under the World Bank assisted project, UP Sodic Land Reclamation Project. The Rae Bareli Kshetriya Gramin Bank (RRB) also took the initiative to link SHGs to its branches. At the time of the survey a few commercial banks were also taking interest in the SBLP in the district, especially Bank of Baroda, State Bank of India, Punjab National Bank, Dena Bank and District Cooperative Bank. These banks have opened savings accounts for the SHGs, but the progress of the linkage has been slow in these banks.

Orissa

The Mcid official in NABARD's regional office in Orissa[9] emphasized that the Government of Orissa understood the importance of the role of SBLP in the development of rural masses and hence it had formed a separate directorate 'Mission Shakti' from March 2001 under the Women and Child Development (W&CD) Department. Under this the Orissa government aims to form 100,000 SHGs by 2005 (25,000 SHGs every year). As of 2003, about 95,000 groups had already been formed in Orissa. This directorate promoted only women SHGs, whereas NABARD promoted both male and mixed SHGs in the state. Mission Shakti worked at the block level through ICDS (Integrated Child Development Society) Department's Community Development Promotion Officer, women supervisor at the local governance (Panchayat) level and an Auxiliary Nursing Midwife at village level.

Special emphasis was given by the state's Chief Minister, in 2003, to involve SHG members in the delivery mechanism. For instance, SHGs of tribal districts like Malkangiri were given the charge to distribute food through the Public Distribution System (PDS) at the village level. This action of the government has been successful as the food now reaches its targeted population (BPL) and black-marketing of items (rice, wheat, sugar and kerosene) are under control. In some districts the SHGs even got the contract for road maintenance.

The selected districts are tribal dominated districts of Orissa. In an interview, NABARD's DDM at Koraput[10] reported that the SBLP was initiated in Koraput district during 1997–98. Koraput has shown a substantial amount of SBLP development and is well placed as compared to other districts. About 500 SHGs are currently under the guidance of NGOs. In total about 6,500 SHGs had been formed in the district, of which about 4,500 have been formed by Panchabati Gramya Bank of Koraput. The Koraput Central Cooperative Bank and commercial banks like State Bank of India (SBI) and Indian Overseas Bank also linked up to the SHGs. Mostly tribal and scheduled caste populations were being targeted in this programme.

The Rayagada district saw the start of the SBLP during year 1995–96. According to the Rayagada NABARD's DDM,[11] by 2001–02 a total of 684 SHGs were credit linked by various banks in the district. By March 2002 about 1,000 SHGs had been linked. Other institutions like RRBs, commercial banks and NGOs also participated in the SBLP. About 17 NGOs were working in the district by 2003 and three of these formed federations. The total number of SHGs promoted in the district was 1,362, while the total number of credit linked SHGs in the district at the time of the interview was 716. Almost all of the government programmes were linked to the SBLP, for instance, Swarnajayanti Gram Swarozgar Yojana, Integrated Tribal Development Programme, Orissa State Financial Development Corporation Programmes (which is mainly an income generation programme) and Panchayat Raj Institution programme.

Notes

1 The Self Help Group-Bank Linkage Programme

1 The National Bank for Agriculture and Rural Development was established as the central bank in 1982.
2 Information extracted from the presentation by Dr K.C. Chakrabarty, Deputy Governor at Skoch Summit on 17 July 2009, titled 'Pushing Financial Inclusion: Issues, Challenges and the Way Forward' (as reported in Srinivasan (2009)).
3 Under priority sector lending the banks were bound to lend 40 per cent of their total bank credit to borrowers from priority sectors, including agriculture, microfinance, small industry, housing and education. Of this, 10 per cent had to be extended to the 'economically weaker sections'.
4 For a detailed discussion on the origins of microfinance in India, refer to Seibel (2010).
5 The post office network handles more than 110 million money orders and administers 114 million savings accounts (Basu 2006).
6 NABARD 1989 studies on Self Help Group of the Rural Poor, Bombay, NABARD.
7 For instance, in the review of rural finance in India it was noticed that most of the rural regional banks were making losses.
8 MYRADA is an NGO in south India, whose action research into credit management groups during 1985–88 was jointly funded by NABARD and Canadian International Development Agency (CIDA).
9 In 1992 NABARD guidelines (Circular Ref. No. NB. DPD. FS. 4631/92-A/91–92, Circular No. DPD/104) had indicated that the SHG size could be between 10 and 25 members. However, there was a legal flaw, as Section 11(2) of the Companies Act forbids any company, association or partnership consisting of more than 20 persons to participate in a business for gain, unless it is registered as a company under Companies Act. Thus, a circular by NABARD on 19 October 1994 (Ref. No. NB.DPD.SHG. 2353/92-A/94–95) advised SHG size be restricted to 20 or less persons for linkage activities.
10 Nair (2005) mentions that NABARD's refinance has been falling in proportion – due to the prevailing low interest rates, high level of liquidity in banks, and/ or because of the banks seeing the programme as a profitable proposition.
11 Interview with Mr K.C. Sahu, District Development Manager, NABARD, Rayagada, Orissa (2003).

12 Loan outstanding is a stock measure of size and standardizes for loan tenor.
13 In SIAS data, 70 per cent of SHGs follow model 2, while 12 per cent and 18 per cent, respectively, follow the first and third models.
14 These federations are different from standard federations due to their smaller size, with their membership being exclusively poor. SHGs also have smaller financial resources and limited human capacity.
15 The High Level Committee to Review Lead Bank Scheme of RBI, chaired by Ms. Usha Thorat, Deputy Governor, RBI (report available at www.rbi.org.in).
16 The bill defines an MFO as any organization that provides microfinance services and includes societies, trusts and cooperative societies. This excludes SHGs and groups of SHGs. The eligible clients are defined as members of any SHG or any group formed to provide microfinance services to categories of people. These categories include: (1) any farmer owning a maximum of two hectares of agricultural land; (2) agricultural cultivators such as oral lessees and share croppers; (3) landless and migrant labourers; (4) artisans and micro entrepreneurs; and (5) women.

2 Impact assessment methodologies and study design

1 This chapter has borrowed liberally from the author's earlier work: Bali Swain and Floro 2012; Bali Swain and Varghese 2009, 2010a, 2011a; Bali Swain and Wallentin 2009.
2 These states are: Rajasthan in the north; Orissa and West Bengal in the east; Madhya Pradesh and Uttar Pradesh in the centre; Gujarat and Maharashtra in the west; Andhra Pradesh, Karnataka and Tamil Nadu in the south.
3 These six states covered about 77 per cent of the bank linked SHGs in India as of 31 March 2002.
4 For a detailed discussion on the selection issues, refer to Armendáriz and Morduch 2010.
5 With panel data, assuming that these unobservable differences are fixed and linear over time, one can eliminate the difference. But as argued above, one faces difficulties with using panel data for SHGs.
6 Selection bias in impact studies on microfinance has been discussed at length in Karlan and Goldberg (2006) and Coleman (1999). More generally, see the recent book by Angrist and von Pischke (2009).
7 Using the totals for the state-wise disaggregated data available in Statement II, SHG–bank linkage – Regional Spread of Physical and Financial Progress up to 31 March 2002, p. 11, in NABARD and microfinance 2001–2002, the total number of Self Help Groups in India was 715,047. This is different from the grand total of 461,478 SHGs as disaggregated data was not available for repeat finance of SHGs at the time of the survey.
8 In some chapters, one observation has been dropped due to missing value.
9 One caveat of this approach is that one needs to assume that the behaviour of the new SHG members has not changed while awaiting loans. An advantage of the slow incubation period of SHGs is that members know for some time the nature of the wait and will not change their behaviour radically as compared to a one time infusion.
10 NABARD's or the bank's decision to form a linkage programme might follow a NGO's choice. We do not have information whether NGOs favour certain villages over others within certain districts.

11 The dropout issue is two-fold (Karlan). In the first case, the incomplete sample bias, dropouts are impacted differently so that an impact assessment does not take into account the whole programme, only better performers. In the second, the attrition bias, the active borrowers are neither failed borrowers nor the stars that chose to graduate. If the failures are more likely to dropout, comparing old and new borrowers overestimates impacts.

12 See Karlan and Goldberg (2006) for a review of the major studies and their methodologies. Another influential paper on microfinance impact is Pitt and Khandker (1998) which relies on Grameen's eligibility rule (although see the recent rebuttal by Morduch and Roodman (2009)).

13 For these 46 households, Bali Swain and Varghese (2009) used the number of the months since they received the first SHG loan for SHGMON.

14 This has been employed by Bali Swain (2012), Bali Swain and Floro (2012) and Bali Swain and Varghese (2010a, 2010b).

15 See Townsend 1995; Dercon 2005; Zimmerman and Carter 2003; and Morduch 2004.

16 Different bandwidths may be used. Bandwidths are smoothing parameters, which control the degree of smoothing for fitting the local linear regression.

17 Vulnerability is defined as a forward-looking, *ex-ante* measure of the household's ability to cope with future shocks and proneness to food insecurity.

3 Reducing poverty and vulnerability

1 This chapter has borrowed liberally from author's earlier work: Bali Swain 2004, 2006, 2012; Bali Swain and Floro 2007, 2012.

2 The differences in the empirical findings arise from varying measures of poverty, different country contexts and types of microfinance organizations being analysed, use of different theoretical models, survey designs and econometric techniques, and/or different time periods covered by the studies.

3 See Glewwe and Hall, 1998; Calvo and Dercon, 2005; Carter and Ikegami, 2007; Ligon and Schechter, 2002; Dercon and Krishnan, 2000; Dercon, 2005.

4 This concept is based on the notion that "future is uncertain, and the possibility of failing to reach some standard of minimal achievement in any well-being dimension is at least a disturbing background noise for some, and an ever-present, oppressing source of stress and dismay for many others" (Calvo, 2008: 1011).

5 Chauduri *et al.* (2002) measure of vulnerability is an unpublished working paper that has been adopted in several studies. Zhang and Wan (2006) explores the effect of livelihood diversification and education on household vulnerability in rural Chinese households. Günther and Harttgen (2009) examine the impact of idiosyncratic and covariate shocks in rural and urban households in Madagascar while the study by Imai *et al.* (2010) analyses the impact of taxation policies on household welfare in China.

6 Surveys of this literature are in Townsend (1995), Bardhan and Udry 1999, Dercon 2005, Zimmerman and Carter (2003), Deaton (1997), Morduch (2004).

7 See Poverty Estimates for 2004–05, Government of India, Press Information Bureau, March 2007.

8 For details on the statistical estimation refer to Chauduri *et al.* (2002).

9 Planning Commission estimates, as accessed on 22 September 2010 www.planningcommission.gov.in/data/datatable/Data0910/tab%2019.pdf.

10 The poverty gap is the average (over all individuals) gap between poor people's living standards and the poverty line. It indicates the average extent to
which individuals fall below the poverty line (if they do). It thus measures how
much would have to be transferred to the poor to bring their income (or consumption) up to the poverty line. The poverty gap however does not capture the
differences in the severity of poverty amongst the poor and ignores "inequality
among the poor". To account for the inequality amongst the poor we calculate
the squared poverty gap index which is defined as the average of the square relative poverty gap of the poor. The squared poverty gap index (Foster-Greer-
Thorbecke Index) is a weighted sum of poverty gaps (as a proportion of the
poverty line), where the weights are the proportionate poverty gaps themselves.

$P_\alpha = \frac{1}{n} \sum_{i=1}^{q} \left(\frac{z - y_i}{z} \right)^\alpha$. The measures are defined for $\alpha \geq 0$, where α is a measure

of the sensitivity of the index to poverty. When $\alpha = 0$, we have the headcount
index (the proportion of the population for whom income (or other measures of
living standard) is less than the poverty line), $\alpha = 1$ is the poverty gap index and
$\alpha = 2$ is the squared poverty gap index.

11 The poverty and vulnerability profile for the SHG and non-SHG member
households is presented here for the sample on common support. Imposing
common support condition in the estimation of the propensity score may
improve the quality of the matches used to estimate ATT (Ichino and Becker,
2002).

12 Both these confounders are "dangerous" confounders, since both the outcome
and the selection effect are positive.

13 The results in this section are based on Bali Swain (2012).

4 Asset creation

1 This chapter borrows liberally from author's earlier work: Bali Swain and Varghese 2009.

2 RBI 2008, p. iii.

3 For this with 218 villages and the available sample size, a regression with 218
dummies is simply infeasible. With aggregation at the district level, any differential impact of the programme due to missing unobservables at the village
level (e.g. village has a more dynamic leader or village has stronger political
connections) cannot be taken into account.

4 The shock dummy = 1 if respondent reports yes to any of the following: social
and religious emergency, failure of crops (includes failure due to lack of rain),
illness in family, loss of work of one of the earning members or natural catas-
trophe (like drought, cyclone or floods). This information was asked for both
2000 and 2003. The two were averaged to create an average shock variable.

5 Since land forms the bulk of assets and land turnover is infrequent in India (see
Pitt-Khandker (1998) for more discussion on this), this variable was the best
choice for initial wealth.

6 This might result from the branching of Indian banks outside the sub-district
(block) headquarters where most of the government offices are located.

7 The unobservables may not make much difference all the time. For instance,
Coleman found that unobservables matter in eight of 72 regressions. In the
specification presented here though the member dummy actually matters (Bali

Swain and Varghese 2009). Without taking membership into account, the impact would be underestimated.

8 The Tobit regressions are the classical Tobit type due to the positive probability of zeroes in the data. Commonly referred to as Type I, the censoring occurs as we move from an aggregate to disaggregate view of assets. Modelling the decision to acquire these specific assets is beyond the scope of this exercise.

9 We also evaluated the impact on 'above average' interest borrowing (as defined as borrowing above 21 per cent). The results for member and SHGMON yielded the following insignificant results, respectively: −6.481 (0.81) and 0.015 (0.12).

10 The breakdown for the components of agricultural income was the following. For agricultural wage income, member: 1.640 (0.82) and SHGMON: −0.073 (1.77). For agricultural profits, member: 4.629 (1.05) and SHGMON: −0.060 (1.18). Tobit regressions on the whole sample yield qualitatively similar results.

11 Carter (2007) arrives at a similar conclusion and notes that the structurally poor may be trapped without the needed minimum capital.

5 Empowering women

1 This chapter has borrowed liberally from author's earlier work: Bali Swain 2006, 2007, 2010; Bali Swain and Wallentin 2009.

2 This strategy was continued in the Tenth Plan (2002–07) with the government commitment to encourage SHGs to act as agents of social change, development and empowerment of women. The SHG programme has emerged across India as one of the most popular strategy for empowering women (India's Finance Minister, P. Chidambaram, 2004).

3 The Millennium Development Goals (MDGs) were agreed at the United Nations Summit in September 2000 by nearly 190 countries. MDG goal 3 aims at promoting gender equality and empowering women.

4 For further discussion on this refer to Armendáriz and Morduch (2010, 179–195).

5 She finds that the effects are even more striking when women have been members of a group for a longer period and especially when greater emphasis has been laid on genuine social intermediation. Social group intermediation had further gradually transformed groups into actors of local institutional change.

6 This methodology lacks the proper treatment of ordinal variables and inappropriately uses the estimated latent scores as observed variables to establish the relationship between credit programme and women's empowerment.

7 For instance, consider that a respondent who is asked the following question: 'What do you do if you are verbally abused in your family?' Her reply is in one of the following categories: 1 (if she resists); 2 (if she submits herself); 3 (if she complains to the group or takes their help); 4 (if she complains to the relatives); 5 (if she warns against such behaviour); and 6 (if she does nothing). In this case the number allocated to the category has no meaning by itself. Even if two different respondents choose the same category 4, we cannot say that their magnitude of resistance to the verbal abuse is the same. It is for these reasons that ordinal variables need to be treated as ordinal variables and require special treatment.

8 It should be noted that although women's empowerment measures for 2000 and 2003 are on the same scale, the origin of the scale is undetermined as the latent variables do not have an origin or a measurement scale.

9 See Kabeer (1999) and Holvoet (2005).

10 Field Survey (Bali Swain, 2003).

11 Refer to Armendáriz and Morduch (2010), McElroy and Horney (1981), Chiappori (1988, 1992), Browning and Chiappori (1998). For a survey on models of allocation within the family, refer to Bergstrom (1996).

12 Several studies have investigated the impact of microfinance on women's rights, especially situation with domestic violence. Hashemi *et al*. (1996) and Kabeer (2001) find that as a result of microfinance, violence against women in Bangladesh has reduced. Whereas, Rahman (1999) finds that domestic violence has increased for Grameen borrowers. Bali Swain (2006) also documents an increase, but argues that the domestic violence is in fact a reaction to the women exerting their rights and reflects the process of empowerment.

13 In rural India, the concept of family is much wider than in the western or even urban context. Second, relationship with the extended family is very close and it is not uncommon for women to take care of all children within the common joint family system, even if they are not their biological mothers. In changes in decision making on some these specific issues are conditioned on some of these events actually occurring. In that sense, these decision making changes record the actual changes that occurred conditioned on the possibility of the event occurring and do not reflect the normative empowered capacity of women.

14 For instance, even though the respondent might not actually have a daughter or might not actually face a decision to send her daughter to school (because her daughter is too old or young), she feels that her involvement in decision making on sending her daughter has increased.

6 Building human capital through training

1 This chapter has borrowed liberally from author's earlier work: Bali Swain and Varghese 2009, 2010a, 2010b, 2011a, 2011b.

2 Until the aforementioned NCAER study, impact studies on SHGs consisted mainly of the Puhazendhi and Badataya study (2002) commissioned by NABARD (India's rural development bank) with 115 members from three states. Their results find that SHG membership significantly increases the asset structure (30 per cent), savings, and annual net income.

3 Public information on the SHG training programme is unavailable. The discussion below is our attempt to distil the information in a concise manner drawing from different sources. Much of this information was provided through visits with NABARD's regional office in Bhubaneswar, Orissa. Some of this information is also available through NABARD circulars.

4 More specifically it includes training on group formation and functioning; functions and qualification of office bearers; rules and regulations; planning, management and monitoring; financial service provisions, conditions and procedures; training of group leaders; and training of book keepers.

5 The MEDP (Microenterprise Development Programme) began only after 2006, which is after our data had been collected. However, it will be discussed more at length in the conclusion.

6 Even with these conditions, Karlan and Valdivia (2009) found many detractors who chose not to attend the training sessions.

7 Interview with Mr Soundara Rajan, Lead District Manager, Indian Bank, Dharamapuri, Tamil Nadu, 2003.

8 For the (new) old SHGs the proportions were the following for the three linkages: Linkage 1 (13.6) 11.2; Linkage 2 (71.7) 72.6; Linkage 3 (14.7) 16.2. A
   two sample *t*-test of proportions confirmed no difference between the two.
9 This may indicate that for villagers other means of transport are more important than buses Bali Swain and Varghese have also estimated separate logit
   regressions for new and old SHG villages. Results were similar for mature
   groups but for new SHGs, the presence of health clinic made training placement less likely.
10 NCAER (2008) also finds that nearly half of all the SHGs have had skill development training. About 35 per cent of the households received training only
   once in 2006 and another 15 per cent have received training multiple times.
11 No impact was found for the following infrastructure variables: distance from
   market, bus-stop, primary healthcare centre, and market.
12 The category 'others' included bank officials, friends and relatives, and anyone
   else. However this represented only 1 per cent of the organizers.

7 Achieving impact and meeting challenges

1 Budget speech available at: http://indiabudget.nic.in/bspeecha.asp.
2 This promotional cost includes cost incurred by SHPI on social mobilization,
   training to animators and SHG members, documentation and linking up SHGs
   with bank.
3 Interview with A.R.K. Raju, Branch Manager, Kalatiya Grameen Bank,
   Warangal, Andhra Pradesh (2003).
4 Interview with Mr D.P. Singh, Chairman, Rae Bareli Khetria Grameen Bank,
   Rae Bareli, Uttar Pradesh (2003).
5 Interview with Mr S.P. Ayalwar, District Co-ordinator, District Central Corporation Bank, Gadchiroli, Maharashtra (2003).
6 Interview with Mr M.I. Ganagi, District General Manager, Mcid, NABARD,
   Regional Office, Pune, Maharashtra (2003).
7 Interview with Mr R.B. Ulke, District General Manager, Chandrapur, Maharashtra, (2003).
8 Interview with Dr Dbesh Roy, District Development Manager, NABARD, Rae
   Bareli, Uttar Pradesh (2003).
9 Interview with Mr K. Anatharaman, Lead District Manager, Indian Bank, Villupuram, Tamil Nadu (2003).

Appendix 1

1 Interview with Deputy General Manager, NABARD (Mcid Section) at the
   Regional Office in Hyderabad (2003).
2 Interview with Mr M.I. Ganagi, Deputy General Manager, Mcid, NABARD,
   Regional Office, Pune, Maharastra (2003).
3 Interview with Mr M.G. Parate, DDM, NABARD, Gadchiroli, Maharastra.
4 Information extracted from interview with Mr R.B. Ulke, District General
   Manager, Chandrapur, Maharashtra (2003).
5 Interview with Mr K. Artha Nareeswaran, DDM, Dharmapuri, Tamil Nadu
   (2003).
6 Interview with Mr S. Srinivasan, DDM, Villupuram, Tamil Nadu (2003).
7 Interview with Mr Pankaj Das, DDM-Mcid NABARD, Lucknow, Uttar
   Pradesh (2003).

8 Interview with Dr Dbesh Roy, DDM, NABARD, Rae Bareli, Uttar Pradesh (2003).
9 Interview with Mr Jagdish Pati, Chief MCID, NABARD Regional Office, Bhubaneswar, Orissa (2003).
10 Interview with Mr Rajkishore Behera, DDM, NABARD, Koraput, Orissa (2003).
11 Interview with Mr K.C. Sahu, DDM, NABARD, Rayagada, Orissa (2003).

Bibliography

Abadie, A. and Imbens, G. 2007. Bias Corrected Matching Estimators for Average Treatment Effects. Working Paper, Department of Economics, Harvard University.

Ackerly, B.A. 1995. Testing the Tools of Development: Credit Programs, Loan Involvement and Women's Empowerment, in *IDS Bulletin 'Getting institutions right for women in development'*, 26(3), 56–68.

Adams, D.W. 1984. Are the Arguments for Cheap Agricultural Credit Sound? in D.W. Adams, D.H. Graham and J.D. von Pischke (eds), *Undermining Rural Development with Cheap Credit*. Westview Press, Boulder, CO.

Adams, D.W. and von Pischke, J.D. 1992. Microenterprise Credit Programs: Déjà Vu. *World Development*, 20(10), 1463–1470.

Ahlin, C. and Jiang, N. 2008. Can Micro-credit Bring Development? *Journal of Development Economics*, 86, 1–21.

Allen, F., Chakrabarti, R. and De, S. 2007. India's Financial System. (27 October 2007).

Amemiya, T. 1997. The Maximum Likelihood Estimator and the Non-linear Three Stage Least Squares Estimator in the General Nonlinear Simultaneous Equation Model. *Econometrica*, 45, 955–968.

Amin, S., Rai, A.S. and Topa, G. 1999. Does Microcredit Reach the Poor and Vulnerable? Evidence from Northern Bangladesh. Working Paper 28, Centre for International Development, Harvard University.

Anderson, S. and Eswaran, M. 2005. What Determines Female Autonomy? Evidence from Bangladesh. Working Paper 101, Bureau for Research and Economic Analysis of Development.

Angrist, J. and von Pischke, J. 2009. *Mostly Harmless Econometrics*. Princeton University Press, Princeton, NJ.

Armendáriz, B. and Morduch, J. 2010. *The Economics of Microfinance*. 2nd edn. MIT Press, Cambridge, Mass.

Ashraf, N., Karlan, D. and Yin, W. 2006. Female Empowerment: Impact of a Commitment Savings Product in Philippines. Center Discussion Paper no. 949, Economic Growth Center, Yale University, New Haven.

Baland, J.-M., Somanathan, R. and Vandewalle, L. 2008. Microfinance Lifespans: A Study of Attrition and Exclusion in Self Help Groups. *India Policy Forum*, 4, 159–210.

Bali Swain, R. 2001. Demand, Segmentation and Rationing in the Rural Credit Markets of Puri. Economic Studies 54, Department of Economics, Uppsala University.

Bali Swain, R. 2002. Credit Rationing in Rural India. *Journal of Economic Development*, 27(2), 1–20.

Bali Swain, R. 2003. Impact of Self Help Groups: Notes from Focus Group Discussions. Unpublished draft, Department of Economics, Uppsala University.

Bali Swain, R. 2004. *Is Microfinance a Good Poverty Alleviation Strategy? Evidence from Impact Assessment.* Sida, Stockholm.

Bali Swain, R. 2006. *Microfinance and Women Empowerment.* Sida, Stockholm.

Bali Swain, R. 2007. Impacting Women through Microfinance. *Dialogue*, Appui au Développement Autonome, 37, 61–82.

Bali Swain, R. 2010. Reducing Poverty and Empowering Women through Microfinance, in S. Chant (ed.), *International Handbook of Gender and Poverty.* Edward Elgar.

Bali Swain, R. 2012. Differential Impact of Microfinance Delivery Mechanism on Vulnerability. *Applied Economics Letters*, 19(8), 1 May 2012, 721–724(4).

Bali Swain, R. and Floro, M. 2007. Effect of Microfinance on Vulnerability, Poverty and Risk in Low Income Households. Working Paper 31, Department of Economics, Uppsala University.

Bali Swain, R. and Floro, M. 2012. Reducing Vulnerability through Microfinance: Evidence from Indian Self Help Group Program. Working Paper 23, Department of Economics, Uppsala University. (Forthcoming in *Journal of Development Studies*).

Bali Swain, R. and Varghese, A. 2009. Does Self Help Group Participation Lead to Asset Creation? *World Development*, 37(10), 1674–1682.

Bali Swain, R. and Varghese, A. 2010a. Being Patient With Microfinance: The Impact of Training on Indian Self Help Groups. Working Paper 22, Department of Economics, Uppsala University.

Bali Swain, R. and Varghese, A. 2010b. Microfinance 'Plus': The Impact of Business Training on Indian Self Help Groups. Working paper 24, Department of Economics, Uppsala University.

Bali Swain, R. and Varghese, A. 2011a. Reassessing the Impact of SHG Participation with Nonexperimental Approaches. *EPW*, 46(11), 50–57.

Bali Swain, R. and Varghese, A. 2011b. Delivery Mechanisms and Impact of Microfinance Training in Indian Self Help Groups. Forthcoming in *Journal of International Development.*

Bali Swain, R. and Wallentin, F.Y. 2009. Does Microfinance Empower Women? Evidence from Self Help Groups in India. *International Review of Applied Economics*, 23(5), 541–556.

Bali Swain, R. and Wallentin, F.Y. 2011. Factors Empowering Women in Indian Self Help Group Program. Forthcoming in *International Review of Applied Economics.*

Banerjee, A. and Duflo, E. 2009. The Experimental Approach to Development Economics. *Annual Review of Economics*, 1, 151–178.

Banerjee, A., Duflo, E., Glennerster, R. and Kinnan, C. 2009. The Miracle of Microfinance? Evidence from a Randomized Evaluation. Working Paper, Department of Economics, MIT.

Bardhan, K. and Klasen, S. 1999. UNDP's Gender-related Indices: A Critical Review. *World Development*, 27, 985–1010.

Bardhan, P. and Udry, C. 1999. *Development Microeconomics*. Oxford University Press, Oxford.

Barnow, B., Cain, G. and Goldberger, A. 1980. Issues in the Analysis of Selectivity Bias, in E. Stromsdorfer and G. Farkas (eds), *Evaluation Studies Review Annual, Vol. 5*. Sage, San Francisco.

Basu, P. 2006. *Improving Access to Finance for India's Rural Poor*. World Bank, Washington, DC.

Basu, P. and Srivastava, P. 2005. *Scaling-up Microfinance for India's Rural Poor*. World Bank Policy Research, Working Paper No. 3646, World Bank, Washington, DC.

Becker, S. and Ichino, A. 2002. Estimation of Average Treatment Effects Based on Propensity Score. *The Stata Journal*, 2, 358–377.

Bergstrom, T. 1996. A Survey of Theories of the Family, in M.R. Rosenzwieg and O. Stark (eds), *Handbook of Population and Family Economics*. North-Holland, Amsterdam.

Beteta, H.C. 2006. What is Missing in Measures of Women's Empowerment? *Journal of Human Development*, 7(2), 221–241.

Bhaduri, A. 1977. On the Formation of Usurious Interest Rates in Backward Agriculture. *Cambridge Journal of Economics*, 1, 341–352.

Browning, M. and Chiappori, P.A. 1998. Efficient Intra-Household Allocations: A General Characterization and Empirical Tests. *Econometrica*, 66, 1241–1278.

Burgess, R. and Pandey, R. 2005. Can Rural Banks Reduce Poverty? Evidence from the Indian Social Banking Experiment. *American Economic Review*, 95(3), 780–795.

Caliendo, M. and Kopeinig, S. 2008. Some Practical Guidance for the Implementation of Propensity Score Matching. *Journal of Economic Surveys*, 22, 31–72.

Calvo, C. 2008. Vulnerability to Multidimensional Poverty: Peru, 1998–2002. *World Development*, 36(6), 1011–1020.

Calvo, C. and Dercon, S. 2005. *Measuring Individual Vulnerability*. University of Oxford Department of Economics Working Paper Series, 229. MIT Press, Cambridge, MA.

Cannon, T., Twigg, J. and Rowell, J. 2003. Social Vulnerability, Sustainable Livelihoods and Disasters. Report to DFID Conflict and Humanitarian Assistance Department (CHAD) and Sustainable Livelihoods Office, London. Available online: www.livelihoods.org/static/tcannon-NN197.htm.

Cardona, O.D. 2004. The Need for Rethinking the Concepts of Vulnerability and Risk from a Holistic Perspective: A Necessary Review and Criticism for Effective Risk Management, in G. Bankoff, G. Frerks and D. Hilhorst (eds), *Mapping Vulnerability: Disasters, Development and People*. Earthscan, London, pp. 37–51.

Carter, M. 2007. What We can Learn from Asset-Based Approaches to Poverty, in C. Moser (ed.), *Reducing Global Poverty: The Case for Asset Accumulation*. Brookings, Washington, DC, pp. 51–61.

Carter, M. and Barrett, C. 2006. The Economics of Poverty Traps and Persistent Poverty: An Asset-Based Approach. *The Journal of Development Studies*, 42(2), 178–199.

Carter, M. and Ikegami, M. 2007. Looking Forward: Theory-based Measures of Chronic Poverty and Vulnerability. CPRS Working Paper No. 94, University of Wisconsin, Madison.

Carter, M., Little, P., Mogues, T. and Negatu, W. 2007. Poverty Traps and the Long-term Consequences of Natural Disasters in Ethiopia and Honduras. *World Development*, 35(5), 835–856.

CGAP. 2006. Community Managed Loan Funds: Which Ones Work? Mimeo, CGAP.

Chauduri, S., Jalan, J. and Suryahadi, A. 2002. Assessing Household Vulnerability to Poverty from Cross Sectional Data: A Methodology and Estimates from Indonesia. Discussion paper 0102–52, Department of Economics, Columbia University.

Cheston, S. and Kuhn, L. 2002. *Empowering Women through Microfinance*. Unpublished Draft, Opportunity International.

Chiappori, P.A. 1988. Rational Household Labour Supply. *Econometrica*, 56, 63–89.

Chiappori, P.A. 1992. Collective Labour Supply and Welfare, *Journal of Political Economy*, 100, 437–467.

Chidambaram, P. 2004. *Budget 2004–2005: Speech of P. Chidambaram, Union Minister of Finance, 8th July 2004.* Available online: http://indiabudget.nic.in/ ub2004–05/bs/speecha.htm (accessed 15 February 2008).

CMF (Centre for Micro Finance). 2010. Access to Finance in Andhra Pradesh, IFMR-CMF, funded by NABARD.

Coleman, B. 1999. The Impact of Lending in Northeastern Thailand. *Journal of Development Economics*, 60, 105–141.

Deaton, A. 1992. *Understanding Consumption*. Clarendon Press, Oxford.

Deaton, A. 1997. *Analysis of Household Surveys: A Microeconomic Approach to Development Policy*. World Bank, Washington, DC.

Deaton, A. 2010. Instruments, Randomization, and Learning about Development. *Journal of Economic Literature*, 48, 424–455.

Dercon, S. 2005. *Vulnerability: a Micro Perspective*. Mimeo, Oxford University.

Dercon, S. and Hoddinott, J. 2005. Health, Shocks and Poverty Persistence, in Stefan Dercon (ed.), *Insurance Against Poverty*. Oxford University Press, Oxford, pp. 124–136.

Dercon, S. and Krishnan, P. 2000. Vulnerability, Seasonality and Poverty in Ethiopia. *Journal of Development Studies*, 36(6), 25–53.

Deshmukh-Ranadive, J. 2003. Placing Gender Equity in the Family Centre Stage: Use of 'Kala Jatha' Theatre, *Economic and Political Weekly*, 26 April 2003.

Dichter, T. and Harper, M. (eds). 2007. *What's wrong with Microfinance?* Practical Action Publishing, Warwickshire.

Dijkstra, G. 2002. Revisiting UNDP's GDI and GEM: Towards an Alternative. *Social Indicators Research*, 57, 301–338.

Doss, C., Grown, C. and Greene, C.D. 2007. *Gender and Asset Ownership*. Mimeo, World Bank, Washington, DC.

Duflo, E. 2003. Grandmothers and Granddaughters: Old Age Pension and Intra-Household Allocation in South Africa. *World Bank Economic Review*, 42, 1–25.

EDA Rural Systems. 2006. *Self Help Groups in India: A Study of Lights and Shades*. EDA Rural Systems, Gurgaon, India.

Ellerman, D. 2007. Microfinance: Some Conceptual and Methodological Problems, in T. Dichter and M. Harper (eds), *What's Wrong with Microfinance*. Practical Action Publishing, Warwickshire.

Estache, A. 2010. A Survey of Impact Evaluations of Infrastructure Projects, Program, and Policies. Working paper, ECARES, Brussels.

Economist Intelligence Unit. 2009. *Global Microscope on the Microfinance Business Environment 2009*. Pilot study.

Fisher, T. and Sriram, M.S. 2002. *Beyond Micro-credit: Putting Development back into Micro-finance*. Vistaar Publications.

Feldbrügge, T. and von Braun, J. 2002. Is the World Becoming a More Risky Place? Trends in Disasters and Vulnerability to Them. Discussion Papers on Development Policy No. 46, Center for Development Research, Bonn.

Frankenberg, E. and Thomas, D. 2001. Measuring Power. FCND Discussion Paper No. 113, International Food Policy Research Institute, Washington, DC.

Ghate, P., Gunaranjan, S., Mahajan, V., Regy, P., Sinha, F. and Sinha, S. 2007. *Microfinance in India: A State of the Sector Report*. Microfinance India, New Delhi.

Glewwe, P. and Hall, G. 1998. Are Some Groups More Vulnerable to Macroeconomic Shocks? Hypothesis Tests Based on Panel Data from Peru. *Journal of Development Economic*, 56(1), 181–206.

Goetz, A.M. and Gupta, R.S. 1996. Who Takes the Credit? Gender, Power, and Control over Loan Use in Rural Credit Programs in Bangladesh. *World Development*, 24(1), 45–63.

Goldberg, N. 2005. *Measuring the Impact of Microfinance: Taking Stock of What We Know*. Mimeo, Grameen Foundation USA.

Guérin, I., Roesch, M. Kumar, S. Venkatasubramanian and Sangare, M. 2009. Microfinance and the Dynamics of Financial Vulnerability: Lessons from rural South India. Rural Microfinance and Employment Project, Working Paper 2009–05, Université de Provence.

Günther, I. and Harttgen, K. 2009. Estimating Households Vulnerability to Idiosyncratic and Covariate Shocks: A Novel Method Applied in Madagascar. *World Development*, 37(7), 1222–1234.

Harper, M. 2002. Self Help Groups and Grameen Bank Groups: What are the differences? in T. Fisher and M.S. Sriram (eds), *Beyond Micro-Credit: Putting Development Back into Microfinance*. Oxfam, UK.

Hashemi S., Schuler, S. and Riley, A. 1996. Rural Credit Programs and Women's Empowerment in Bangladesh. *World Development*, 24(4), 635–653.

Heckman, J. 1992. Randomization and Social Policy Evaluation, in C. Manski and I. Garfinkel (eds), *Evaluating Welfare and Training Programs*. Harvard University Press, Cambridge, MA.

Heckman, J. and Hotz, J. 1989. Alternative Methods for Evaluating the Impact of Training Programs (with discussion). *Journal of the American Statistical Association*, 84(804), 862–874.

Heckman, J., Ichimura, H. and Todd, P. 1997. Matching as an Econometric Evaluation Estimator: Evidence from Evaluating a Job Training Programme. *Review of Economic Studies*, 64, 605–654.

Heitzmann, K., Canagarajah, R.S. and Siegel, P.B. 2002. Guidelines for Assessing the Sources of Risk and Vulnerability. Social Protection Discussion Paper Series, Social Protection Unit, World Bank, Washington, DC.

Holvoet, N. 2005. The Impact of Microfinance on Decision-making Agency: Evidence from South India. *Development and Change*, 36(1), 75–102.

Hulme, D. and McKay, A. 2005. *Identifying and Measuring Chronic Poverty*. Mimeo, Chronic Poverty Research Center, Manchester.

Ichino, A. and Becker, S. 2002. Estimation of Average Treatment Effects Based on Propensity Score. *The Stata Journal*, 2, 358–377.

Ichino, A., Mealli, F. and Nannicini, T. 2007. From Temporary Help Jobs to Permanent Employment: What Can We Learn from Matching Estimators and their Sensitivity? *Journal of Applied Econometrics*, 23(3), 305–327.

Imai, K.S., Wang, X. and Kang, W. 2010. Poverty and Vulnerability in Rural China: Effects of Taxation, *Journal of Chinese Economic and Business Studies*, 8(4), 399–425.

Imbens, G. 2004. Non Parametric Estimation of Average Treatment Effects Under Exogeneity: A Review. *The Review of Economics and Statistics*, 86(1), 4–29.

Isern, J., Prakash, L.B. *et al.* 2007. *Sustainability of Self Help Groups in India: Two Analyses*. CGAP, Washington, DC.

Jha, R. and Dang, T. 2009. Vulnerability to Poverty in Select Central Asian Countries. *European Journal of Comparative Economics*, 6(1), 17–50.

Johnson, S. 2005. Gender Relations, Empowerment and Microcredit: Moving on from a Lost Decade. *European Journal of Development Research*, 17(2), 224–248.

Jöreskog, K.G. 2002. *Structural Equation Modeling with Ordinal Variables using LISREL*. Scientific Software International, Chicago, IL.

Kabeer, N. 1999. Resources, agency, achievements: reflections on the measurement of women's empowerment. *Development and Change*, 30(3), 435–464.

Kabeer, N. 2001. Conflicts Over Credit: Re-evaluating the Empowerment Potential of Loans to Women in Rural Bangladesh. *World Development*, 29(1), 63–84.

Kabeer, N. 2005. Is Microfinance a 'Magic Bullet' for Women's Empowerment? Analysis of Findings from South Asia. *Economic and Political Weekly*, 29 October 2005.

Kamanou, G. and Morduch, J. 2005. Measuring Vunerability to Poverty, in Stefan Dercon (ed.), *Insurance Against Poverty*. Oxford University Press, Oxford.

Karlan, D. 2001. Microfinance Impact Assessments: The Perils of Using New Members as a Control Group. *Journal of Microfinance*, 3, 76–85.

Karlan, D. 2007. Impact Evaluation for Microfinance: Review of Methodological Issues. Poverty Reduction and Economic Management (PREM), Doing Impact Evaluation, Discussion Paper 7, World Bank, Washington, DC.

Karlan, D. and Goldberg, N. 2006. The Impact of Microfinance: A Review of Methodological Issues. Working paper, Yale University.

Karlan, D. and Valdivia, M. 2009. Teaching Entrepreneurship: Impact of Business Training on Microfinance Clients and Institutions. Working paper, Yale University.

Karmakar, K.G. 1999. *Rural Credit and Self-help Groups: Micro-finance Needs and Concepts in India*. Sage Publications, New Delhi.

Khandker, S. 2005. Microfinance and Poverty: Evidence Using Panel Data from Bangladesh. *World Bank Economic Review*, 19, 263–286.

Khandker, S. 1998. *Fighting Poverty with Microcredit: Experience in Bangladesh*. Oxford University Press, New York.

Krishna, A. 2003. Social Capital, Community Driven Development, and Empowerment: A Short Note on Concepts and Operations. Working Paper 33077, World Bank, Washington, DC.

LaLonde, R.J. 1995. The Promise of Public Sector-sponsored Training Programs. *Journal of Economic Perspectives*, 9(2), 149–168.

Leuven, E. and Sianesi, B. 2009. PSMATCH2: Stata module to perform full Mahalanobis and propensity score matching, common support graphing, and covariate imbalance testing. Statistical Software Components S432001, Boston College Department of Economics.

Ligon, E. and Schechter, L. 2002. Measuring Vulnerability: The Director's Cut. UN/WIDER Working paper.

Ligon, E. and Schechter, L. 2003. Measuring Vulnerability. *The Economic Journal*, 113(486), 95–102.

Ligon, E. and Schechter, L. 2004. Evaluating Different Approaches to Estimating Vulnerability. Social Protection Discussion Paper 0201, World Bank, Washington, DC.

Mahajan, V. 2007. *From Microcredit to Livelihood Finance. What's Wrong with Microfinance?* Practical Action Publishing, Warwickshire.

Mahajan, V. and Gupta, B.R. 2003. *Microfinance in India: Banyan Tree and Bonsai*. World Bank, Washington, DC.

Malhotra, A. and Mather, M. 1997. Do Schooling and Work Empower Women in Developing Countries? Gender and Domestic Decisions in Sri Lanka. *Sociological Forum*, 12(4), 599–630.

Manser, M. and Murray, B. 1980. Marriage and Household Decision-Making: A Bargaining Analysis. *International Economic Review*, 21(1), 31–44.

Mayoux, L. 1997. *The Magic Ingredient? Microfinance and Women's Empowerment*. Briefing Paper prepared for Micro Credit Summit, Washington, DC.

Mayoux, L. 1999. Questioning Virtuous Spirals: Micro-Finance and Women's Empowerment in Africa. *Journal of International Development*, 11(7), 957–984.

Mayoux, L. 2001. Tackling the Down Side: Social Capital, Women's Empowerment and Micro-Finance in Cameroon. *Development and Change*, 32.

McCulloch, N. and Baulch, B. 2000. Simulating the Impact of Policy upon Chronic and Transitory Poverty in Rural Pakistan. *Journal of Development Studies*, 36(6), 100–130.

McElroy, M. and Horney, M.J. 1981. Nash-Bargained Household Decisions: Toward a Generalization of the Theory of Demand. *International Economic Review*, 22, 333–349.

Meyer, R. 2002. Microfinance, Poverty Alleviation, and Improving Food Security: Implications for India, in R. Lal (ed.), *Food Security and Environmental Quality*. CRC Press, Boca Raton, FL.

Meyer, R. 2007. Measuring the Impact of Microfinance, in T. Ditcher and M. Harper (eds), *What's Wrong with Microfinance?* Practical Action Publishing, Warwickshire.

Moghadam, V. and Senftova, L. 2005. Measuring Women's Empowerment: Participation and Rights in Civil, Political, Social, Economic, and Cultural Domains. *International Social Science Journal*, 57(2), 389–412.

Morduch, J. 1998. Does Microfinance Really Help the Poor? New Evidence from Flagship Programs in Bangladesh. Mimeo, New York University.

Morduch, J. 1999 The Microfinance Promise. *Journal of Economic Literature*, 37, 1569–1614.

Morduch, J. 2000. The Microfinance Schism. *World Development*, 28, 617–629.

Morduch, J. 2004. Consumption Smoothing Across Space: Testing Theories of Risk-Sharing in the ICRISAT Study Region of South India, in Stefan Dercon (ed.), *Insurance against Poverty*. Oxford University Press, Oxford, pp. 38–57.

Morduch, J. and Roodman, D. 2009. The Impact of Microcredit on the Poor in Bangladesh: Revisiting the Evidence. Working paper, Center for Global Development.

Morduch, J. and Rutherford, S. 2003. Microfinance: Analytical Issues for India. Background paper prepared for the World Bank. World Bank, Washington, DC.

NABARD. 1991. *Annual Report 1990–91. Credit Needs of the Rural Poor: Role of Self Help Groups and Their Linkages with Formal Credit Institutions.* NABARD, Mumbai.

NABARD. 1992. *Guidelines for the Pilot Project for Linking Banks with Self Help Groups*, NB.DPD.FS.4631/92-A/91–92, Circular No. DPD/104. NABARD, Mumbai.

NABARD. 2000. Circular NB.mCID/H-1626/SHG-1/1999–2000, 28 February 2000. NABARD, Mumbai.

NABARD. 2003. *Progress of SHG–Bank Linkage in India 2002–2003*. NABARD, Mumbai.

NABARD. 2006. *Progress of SHG–Bank Linkage in India: 2005–06*. Working Paper, NABARD, Mumbai.

NABARD. 2009. *Status of Microfinance in India: 2008–2009*. NABARD, Mumbai.

NABARD. 2011. *Annual Report 2010–2011*. NABARD, Mumbai.

Nair, A. 2005. Sustainability of Microfinance Self Help Groups in India: Would Federating Help? *World Bank Policy Research Working Paper No. 3516*, World Bank, Washington, DC.

NCAER (National Council of Applied Economic Research). 2008. *Impact and Sustainability of SHG Bank Linkage Programme*. New Delhi.

Nussbaum, M., Kumar, A. and Miehlbradt, A. 2005. *Integrating Microenterprise into Markets: The Case of EDA's Leather Subsector Project in India*. Seep Network Case Study #2, Seep Network.

Parpart, Jane, Rai, Shirin and Staudt, Kathleen. 2002. Rethinking Em(power)ment, Gender and Development: An Introduction, in Jane Parpart, Shirin Rai and Kathleen Staudt (eds), *Rethinking Empowerment: Gender and Development in a Global/Local World*. Routledge, London, pp. 3–21.

Pitt, M. 1999. Reply to Jonathan Morduch's 'Does Microfinance Really Help the Poor'? New Evidence from Flagship Programs in Bangladesh. Mimeo, Brown University.

Pitt, M. and Khandker, S.R. 1998. The Impact of Group-Based Credit Programs on Poor Households in Bangladesh: Does the Gender of the Participant Matter? *Journal of Political Economy*, 106, 958–996.

Pitt, M., Khandker, S.R. and Cartwright, J. 2006. Empowering women with microfinance: evidence from Bangladesh. *Economic Development and Cultural Change*, 54(4), 791–831.

Planning Commission. 2002. *Tenth Five Year Plan 2002–2007*, Government of India, New Delhi, pp. 239.

Prowse, M. 2003. *Towards a Clearer Understanding of 'Vulnerability' in Relation to Chronic Poverty*. CPRC Working Paper No. 24, University of Manchester.

Puhazendhi, V. and Badataya, K. 2002. *SHG–Bank Linkage Programme for Rural Poor: An Impact Assessment*. Paper presented at seminar on SBLP at New Delhi, 25–26 November. National Bank for Agriculture and Rural Development, Mumbai.

Puhazhendi, V. and Satyasai, K.J.S. 2000. *Microfinance for Rural People: An Impact Evaluation*. Department of Economic Anaysis and Research, NABARD, Mumbai.

Purushottaman, S. 1998. *The Empowerment of Women in India: Grassroots Women's Networks and the State*, Sage Publications, New Delhi.

Pulley, R. 1989. *Making the Poor Creditworthy: A Case of the Integrated Rural Development Program in India*. World Bank Discussion Paper 58. World Bank, Washington, DC.

Rahman, A. 1999. Microcredit Initiatives for Equitable and Sustainable Development: Who Pays? *World Development*, 27(1).

Ramakrishna, R.V. 2006. Management Information Systems (MIS): SHG Bank Linkage Programme. Mimeo, GTZ, New Delhi.

RBI (Reserve Bank of India). 1954. *All India Rural Credit Survey of 1951–52*.

RBI (Reserve Bank of India). 1981–82. *All India Debt and Investment Survey*.

RBI (Reserve Bank of India). 1991. *Improving access of rural poor to banking: Role of intervening agencies – Self Help Groups*. Circular issued to all Scheduled Commercial Banks.

RBI (Reserve Bank of India). 1996. Circular RPCD. PL. BC./120/04.09.22/95–96, 2 April 1996.

RBI (Reserve Bank of India). 2000. Circular RPCD. PL. BC.62/04.09.01/99-2000, Mumbai, February 2000.

RBI (Reserve Bank of India). 2008. *Rangarajan Committee on Financial Inclusion*.

Rosenbaum, P. 1987. Sensitivity Analysis to Certain Permutation Inferences in Matched Observational Studies. *Biometrika*, 74(1), 13–26.

Rosenbaum, P. 2002. *Observational Studies*. 2nd edn, Springer, New York.

Rosenbaum, P. and Rubin, D. 1983. Assessing Sensitivity to an Unobserved Binary Covariate in an Observational Study with Binary Outcome. *Journal of the Royal Statistical Society*, Series B, 45, 212–218.

Sa-Dhan 2001. *Micro-finance regulation in India*. Sa-Dhan, New Delhi.

Satish, P. 2001. Institutional Alternatives for Promotion of Microfinance: Self-Help Groups in India. *Journal of Microfinance*, 3, 50–79.

Seibel, H.D. 2001. *SHG Banking: A Financial Technology for Reaching Marginal Areas and the Very Poor*. University of Cologne, Cologne.

Seibel, H.D. 2006. From Informal Microfinance to Linkage Banking: Putting Theory into Practice, and Practice into Theory. *European Dialogue*, 36 (September).

Seibel, H.D. 2010. Old and New Worlds of Microfinance, in A. Goenka and D. Henley (eds), *Southeast Asia's Credit Revolution from Moneylenders to Microfinance*. Routledge, Abingdon.

Seibel, H.D. and Dave, H.R. 2002. *Commercial Aspects of Self-Help Group Banking in India: A Study of Bank Transaction Costs*. Mumbai, National Bank for Agriculture and Rural Development.

Sinha, F., Tankha, A. *et al.* 2009. *Microfinance Self Help Groups in India: Living Up to Their Promise?* Practical Action Publishing.

Schuler, S., Hashemi, S. and Riley, A. 1997. The Influence of Women's Changing Roles and Status on Bangladesh's Fertility Transition: Evidence from a Study of Credit Programs and Contraceptive Use. *World Development*, 25(4), 563–575.

Sharma, S. 2005. *Factor Immobility and Regional Inequality: Evidence from a Credit Shock in India*. Mimeo, Department of Economics, Yale University.

Smith, J. and Todd, P. 2005. Does Matching Address Lalonde's Critique of Non-experimental Estimators? *Journal of Econometrics*, 125, 305–353.

Srinivasan, N. 2009. *Microfinance in India: State of the Sector Report*. SAGE, New Delhi.

Srinivasan, N. 2010. *Microfinance in India: State of Sector Report*. SAGE, New Delhi.

Srinivasan, N. 2011. *Microfinance in India: State of Sector Report*. SAGE, New Delhi.

Stromquist, N. 2002. Education as a Means for Empowering Women, in J. Parpart, S. Rai and K. Staudt (eds), *Rethinking Empowerment: Gender and Development in a Global/Local World*, Routledge, London, pp. 22–38.

Summer-Effler, E. 2002. The Micro Potential for Social Change: Emotion, Consciousness, and Social Movement Formation. *Sociological Theory*, 20(1), 41–60.

Tankha, A. 2002. *Self-Help Groups as Financial Intermediaries in India: Cost of Promotion, Sustainability, and Impact*. ICCO, The Netherlands.

Tedeschi, G. 2008. Overcoming Selection Bias in Microcredit Impact Assessments: A Case Study in Peru. *Journal of Development Studies*, 44, 504–518.

Tesoriero, F. 2005. Strengthening Communities through Women's Self-help Groups in South India. *Community Development Journal*, 41(3), 321–333.

Townsend, J. 1999. Power from Within: Getting Out of That House, in J. Townsend, E. Zapata, J. Rowlands, P. Alberti and M. Mercado (eds), *Women and Power: Fighting Patriarchies and Poverty*. Zed Books, London.

Townsend, R.M. 1995. Consumption Insurance: An Evaluation of Risk-Bearing Systems in Low-Income Economies. *Journal of Economic Perspectives*, 9, 83–102.

World Bank. 2000. *World Development Report 2000/2001: Attacking Poverty.* World Bank and Oxford University Press, Washington, DC and New York.

World Bank. 2001. *Engendering Development: Through Gender Equality in Rights, Resources, and Voice.* World Bank Policy Research Report. World Bank and Oxford University Press, Washington, DC and New York.

World Bank. 2009. *World Development Report 2008: Agriculture for Development.* World Bank, Washington, DC.

World Bank and National Council of Applied Economic Research. 2003. *Scaling up Access to Finance for India's Rural Poor: India Rural Finance Access Survey.* New Delhi, Finance and Private Sector Development Unit, South Asia Region, World Bank, Washington, DC.

Zhang, Y. and Wan, G. 2006. An Empirical Analysis of Household Vulnerability in Rural China. *Journal of the Asia Pacific Economy*, 11(2), 196–211.

Zimmerman, F. and Carter, M. 2003. Asset Smoothing, Consumption Smoothing and the Reproduction of Inequality Under Risk and Subsistence Constraints. *Journal of Development Economics*, 71, 233–260.

Index

Page numbers in *italics* denote tables, those in **bold** denote figures.

violence 18, 67, 119n12
von Braun, J. 32
von Pischke, J. 115n6
von Pischke, J.D. 101
vulnerability 29, 30; definitions 31, 33,
  95; and delivery mechanism 43–4;
  ex-ante measure 32, 33, 95, 116n17;
  future food consumption 38, 39; and
  SBLP 31, 32, 39, 42; and Self Help
  Groups 95–6; threshold 39; *see also*
  poverty and vulnerability

Wallentin, F.Y. 29, 63, 65, 66, 68–9,
  71–2, 79–80, 81
Wan, G. 116n5
Warangal district, Andhra Pradesh 109
West Bengal 115n2
women, empowerment of 29, 59–82,
  95, 96–7; conceptual framework 66;
  defining in South Asian context

63–4; direct and indirect strategies
  60, 61; economic factor, significance
  79, 80; factors empowering women
  70–80, **73**, *74–8*, 79; measuring
  64–6; microfinance and
  empowerment 59–62; path diagram
  66, **67**, **73**; and SBLP 59; social
  attitudes 79–80; structural equation
  model 71–2; through Self Help
  Groups 66–70, 71, 95; variables 66,
  72, *74–8*
Women and Child Development
  (W&CD) Department, Orissa 112
World Bank 57–8

yield risks 30

Zhang, Y. 116n5
Zimmerman, F. 116n6, 116n15

For Product Safety Concerns and Information please contact our
EU representative GPSR@taylorandfrancis.com Taylor & Francis
Verlag GmbH, Kaufingerstraße 24, 80331 München, Germany